Responses from Readers

"I bought this book at an airport terminal while I was waiting for a flight with my fiancé. After we read and discussed the first two chapters, he committed to dealing with personal issues that he had been avoiding for years. Thank you!"

Ashley Smith, Business Graduate Student

"I found *The Power of Balance* to be an incredible synthesis of knowledge. Its unique approach has already been helping me make changes in my life. I particularly liked Jack's autobiographical style–that helped tie it all together for me."

Michael Evert, Computer Program Designer

"The 'Shadow' section of *The Power of Balance* greatly helped me deal with issues that have been sabotaging me all my life."

Mary Wheatly, Management Consultant

"Reading *The Power of Balance* helped me realize that although I was financially successful, I was spiritually bankrupt. I liked the book's business-like approach to everyday spirituality."

Peter Townsend, Owner, Software Company

"I've done a lot of self-help and self-development programs. *The Power of Balance* gave me a new way to find answers that I have long been searching for. I'm also very impressed with Jack Beauregard's courage in writing this book."

Ann Michael, Personal Coach

About the Author

Jack Beauregard was the CEO of a multi–million dollar national orthopedic products company in 1982, when he received the mystical message that he should take the gifts which had brought him conventional success, use them to deepen his inner life, then share his spiritual journey with others.

In the years that followed—guided by intuition and love—Jack combined intense internal work with the wisdom teachings of the world's great spiritual traditions and the latest discoveries in modern science, to develop an extremely practical and effective program for self–healing and meaningful personal transformation.

The Power of Balance describes Jack Beauregard's extraordinary personal story and unique process for self–transformation.

The Power of Balance

*Seven Principles for
Transforming
Mind, Spirit, and Self*

Jack Beauregard

Innervision Press
Cambridge, Massachusetts

Published by:

Innervision Press
5 Warwick Pk.
Cambridge, MA 02140
Toll-free number: 888-617-6715

The Power of Balance™ is a federally registered trademark of Innervisions Associates, Inc.

Copyright 2001 by Jack Beauregard.
First Printing 2000
Second Printing 2001

Beauregard, Jack
     The Power of Balance™ / Jack Beauregard.– –1st ed.
     p. cm.
     Includes bibliographical references.
     ISBN 0-9662362-0-3

     1. Self–help techniques. 2. Cosmology.
     3. Self-perception. 4. Emotions and cognition
     I. Title.

     BF632.B42 1998   158.1
                              QBI98-89

Dedication

To Judy:

A promise made, a promise kept.

To Maureen:

For her unconditional love, her financial support and her copy editing, which in many ways have made this book possible.

To Kathleen Zagata:

A professional soulmate whose support and faith have been an inspiration to me over the years.

To Barbara Brandt:

Whose editorial work, insights, and guidance transformed this book.

To my children Amy and Justin:

May this book help make a better world for you and your children.

Acknowledgments

I wish to thank the following people in chronological order, not in order of importance:

To Pat Thatcher–Hill, whose love provided much needed support when my life was between the three b's: books and baby bottles.

To Michelle at the Theological Library and Bookstore, who provided the first forum for bringing the Balanced Paradigm public.

To all the people who have been associated with Innervisions over the years, whose belief in me reaffirmed the value of the balanced model and philosophy of life.

To all the seekers of truth who have made this book possible.

Contents

Introduction

I have always felt there is a deeper meaning to life than achieving material success. When I was living the American Dream, president of a nationally successful medical supply company, with a big house, cars, yacht, etc., I still felt a persistent inner emptiness. Religion as I knew it—that is, the conventional, institutionalized religion of my childhood, which focused on sin and guilt and emphasized our separation from God—did not answer my need.

Like many people who value success and self–improvement, I spent many years trying "positive thinking." As a long time sales trainer with major medical corporations, I knew how important positive thinking was for professional success. But after reading dozens of positive self–help books, attending self–help seminars, and listening to self–help tapes, I still had not achieved any fundamental changes in my personal life. Why was I spending so much time trying to be positive, yet still doing negative things?

Then I read an article by the widow of the famous self–help guru Dale Carnegie, who revealed that he could never finish the last chapter of his classic best–selling book *How to Make Friends and Influence People*. The truth was that Dale Carnegie could not write about what to do when things go wrong.

I've had plenty of things go wrong in my life. I was achieving fantastic material and career success but still feeling a deep emptiness inside. Then my marriage broke up, which devastated me. After that, I miraculously met and married my soulmate Judy, and we shared several incredible years together before we learned that Judy had terminal cancer. Not only did I lose my beloved wife, but I also had to give up my nationally successful business and raise our two–year–old son Justin by myself and essentially start my entire life over.

By this time I had begun to recognize that my life had long been driven by numerous self–defeating traits which caused serious negative consequences both for me and the people I was involved with. Since I would be solely responsible for Justin's early upbringing and did not want to pass these negative traits onto my son, I realized that I would have to transform myself deeply in both thought and action.

The answers and transformation I sought came from a spiritual quest that I began 21 years ago. As part of this quest I read widely in psychological, spiritual, historical, and scientific literature.* Since I live in the Boston area I also attended the Harvard Divinity School for several years as a non–degreed student, where I was able to meet and learn from scholars and spiritual representatives from a wide variety

---

*The following books were especially influential in helping me understand the new paradigm and develop my transformational worldview: Wayne Dyer, *The Sky's the Limit* and *Pulling Your Own Strings*; the *Cosmos,* PBS series and book, Carl Sagan; Dr. Richard Maurice Bucke, *Cosmic Consciousness*; Marilyn Ferguson, *The Aquarian Conspiracy*; William James, *The Varieties of Religious Experience*; *The Power of Myth,* PBS series and book, Bill Moyers and Joseph Campbell; Carl Jung, *Man and His Symbols*; Robert Ornstein, *The Psychology of Consciousness*; Fritjof Capra, *The Tao of Physics* and *The Turning Point;* Gyorgy Doczi, *The Power of Limits*; Matthew Fox, *Original Blessing*; Fred Alan Wolf and Bob Toben, *Space–Time and Beyond*; Dr. Andrew Morrison, *Culture of Shame*; Erich Jantsch, *The Self-Organizing Universe*; Rudiger Dahlke, *Mandalas of the World*; J.C. Smuts, *Holism and Evolution*; Brian Swimme, *The Universe Is a Green Giant*; and Thomas Berry, *The Dream of the Earth..*

of religious and spiritual traditions. Through my wife Judy and other spiritually–guided people I had already begun to broaden my experiences, which gave me a more spiritual understanding about what I should be doing in life. As new insights came to me through this broad learning process, I used my courage and strong sense of motivation to push forward with the changes I needed to make.

The first major lesson I learned through this process was that before I could become "positive" I had to accept the negatives in my life, especially the negative characteristics buried deep within my own personality. These traits, which I believe are not innate, but learned, constitute what is often called a "Shadow." By becoming aware of and accepting my Shadow fully, I gradually freed myself from its unrecognized domination over my life. Only then could I begin to create positive alternatives inside of myself to balance my long–held negative traits and beliefs. I accept that I will never be completely free of my Shadow. Life is a process, and I will always be participating in the process of catching my Shadow's influence over my feelings and actions. But the more awareness I have of my Shadow and its effects, the greater my freedom to live more fully with my authentic inner self.

Through my quest I also learned that each of us is born with an authentic inner self—or soul—which is aware of its connection to the Divine Creative Force of the universe. You may prefer to call this force God, or whatever term feels best to you. I believe that for most of us, our connection to our inner soul, and therefore our connection to the creative power of the universe was gradually clouded over, both by the emotional and relational traumas of our lives and by the negative and self–limiting beliefs we learned—first from our parents and family, then from our teachers and religious authorities, and finally from the broader society and culture, including our political leaders and the media.

Finally, I discovered that the process of *dynamic balance* is essential for self-transformation and personal fulfillment. From the latest scientific discoveries about the nature of life and the universe, I learned that balance is not a static state, but a dynamic process created through the continued interaction of seemingly separate but in fact mutually complementary and interconnected opposites. By applying the Power of Balance to every aspect of my life, I have been able to participate in a dynamic process of change and growth, living my authentic self in a complex and ever-changing world and responding creatively to both its technological and material advances and its deep spirituality and inner meaning.

The world is now going through a time of great human, social, and spiritual evolution. Many people say that as we enter the 21st century we are going through a "paradigm shift." Two older cultural paradigms still shape our lives today. One is the "Traditionalist" paradigm, which reveres rigid control and authority, often justified by reference to an all–powerful, distant, and harshly judgmental God. The second is the "Modernist" or "Materialist" paradigm, which worships the myth of technological and material progress. This paradigm is justified by references to Newtonian science, which teaches that we are basically collections of mindless, spiritless matter; that the world is like a machine, best understood by breaking it down into its smallest separate parts; and that something is real only if it can be measured numerically. The "Traditionalist" and "Materialist" paradigms are limited and destructive, each in its own way.[1]

The emerging paradigm, sometimes called the "Wholistic" paradigm or "Integral Culture," seeks to integrate many aspects of our lives which the two earlier paradigms viewed as separate. For example, the new paradigm understands that as individuals and as a society we need to value both our masculine and our feminine aspects. We are now beginning to understand that each of us is made up of mind, body, emotions, and spirit, all interacting and all needing to be recognized and nurtured. Earlier paradigms taught that people should relate to each other either through dualistic models of superiors and inferiors (e.g., men over women, priests over lay people, royalty over commoners); or as isolated individuals connected only by monetary contracts whose purpose was to maximize the financial bottom line. But in the emerging paradigm we are coming to understand that every one of us is different, yet we are all interconnected, and we can relate best by honoring our own and each other's wholeness and uniqueness. Finally, we are seeing the emergence of a "New Science," which emphasizes the interconnectedness, oneness, and wholeness of the universe, and includes intelligence and spirituality as an integral part of scientific understanding.

Because so many aspects of this emerging paradigm are based on achieving a new balance between what were formally seen as isolated or oppositional aspects of reality, I prefer to call this emerging integrative worldview the "Balanced Paradigm." (This is yet another example of the Power of Balance.)

In order to apply the insights and discoveries of this emerging Balanced Paradigm to my own life, I developed a set of principles and a system of exercises, applications, and insights for self–transformation. As I continued to work with the Balanced Paradigm and the Power of

Balance, my own life slowly became transformed.

I began to move beyond my negative conditioning and self–limiting beliefs, gaining an inner feeling of balance and wholeness and starting to live from the deepest part of my being. Gradually the world around me changed from a source of hostility, even terror, to a place of fulfillment and joy. Instead of treating other people as objects and using them while simultaneously feeling isolated, I began to treat both myself and other people with respect, and increasingly my life became filled with satisfying relationships and love. I moved beyond my focus on external standards and material values, and came to understand that I, and every one of us, are inherently connected to the cosmic creative force of the universe and have a spiritual purpose in life. And I discovered that as I gave up my need for control, I could allow miracles to happen in my life.

I believe that our world is now at a crucial turning point. The old paradigms and the faulty lessons they teach us about ourselves and the world are threatening both human well–being and the future of the earth itself. By teaching us that we are essentially separate from each other, we are encouraged to be hostile, cruel, and violent towards each other. By teaching us to despise ourselves and to worship material success, we are drowning in greed and competitiveness and gobbling up the earth's resources at a dangerous rate.

I wrote this book because I feel a passionate commitment to speak out for the emerging Balanced Paradigm. I want people to know that we can make real and lasting changes in our lives. We can break out of the cycle of passing on negative and self–limiting beliefs, and instead become who we are really meant to be—and help our children grow into who they are really meant to be. I want to share the messages of balance, centeredness, and wholeness; encourage people to discover our innate connection with divine creation, so we can become open both to the deepest parts of our own beings and to the spirituality and gifts of the cosmos.

Not only will such changes help us live happier lives filled with meaning and purpose. As each of us reconnects to our original core, reestablishes our wholeness, and opens to our higher spirituality, I believe we will bring the divine creative spirit into our everyday lives, transforming ourselves, our relations to those we love, to the larger society, and with the earth. Applying the Power of Balance will enable us to transform ourselves so we can become more effective and loving participants in the process of life, both in our personal lives and in our larger world.

Since my personal journey was where I first learned about and applied the Power of Balance for self–transformation, I will tell my story more fully. Next I will describe the new scientific discoveries and changing cultural and historical paradigms which provide a broader background for my story and transformation. Later chapters explain each principle of the Balanced Paradigm, along with exercises which help you to create meaningful, permanent changes in your life.

My job in this book is to share with you what I have learned during my quest toward creating permanent, transformational changes for myself. It is your job to do your own inner work in order to complete your own quest. Ultimately, *you* are your own "guru," and all the answers you are looking for are already inside you, just waiting to be discovered.

Chapter 1

Making the Journey
of Personal Transformation

I grew up in Haverhill, Massachusetts, one of the three cities along the Merrimack River where the American Industrial Revolution began. When I was born, I almost died, since the local hospital had no idea what was wrong with me. (In fact, when I was in the hospital I was baptized three times by three different priests, because my survival seemed so uncertain.) I was rushed to Children's Hospital in Boston where doctors diagnosed the problem as a calcium deficiency, the result of my mother not drinking milk during her pregnancy because she thought the milkman was dirty. My first three months of life were lived inside an incubator.

My father was away in the Army, stationed in France in 1945, when I was born. He had to leave school during the seventh grade to support his family, and earned his living first as a shipper in one of the many shoe factories in Haverhill, then as an electrician.

My mother was a woman ahead of her time. She achieved the highest level that any woman had ever reached in Bell Laboratories, and whenever she encountered the "glass ceiling," she went directly to corporate headquarters in New York City and kept breaking through to new levels.

My parents did not enact the typical gender roles of the times. My mother was the "male" in the family, since career and achievements were her main focus in life, and my father was the "female," since he provided me with love and nurturing. My mother used anger in order to maintain control. Many nights during supper she would attack my father and he would simply accept it. I would often end up in arguments with my mother, fighting my father's battles.

I was an only child raised in an extremely strong Irish Catholic culture, with the church the core of my parent's social environment. Achievement was the most important thing in my life. I attended a Catholic grammar school and high school and was a member of the Catholic Youth Organization and church–sponsored Boy Scouts. By the age of 14 I had become an Eagle Scout (the highest award in Boy Scouting) and also received the *Alter Teri Diem*, the highest Catholic Scouting award. During my senior year in high school I decided to enter the seminary, largely because of Father Laport, who was a major influence during my teen years.

Father Laport was a Catholic priest from Haverhill who worked with the youth gangs in South Boston. Whenever he returned to Haverhill to visit his mother, he would hang around with us teenagers, play basketball, or jump into a car with a bunch of us and go to a local beach. Father Laport did not talk pious dogma. He was a man's man. When I was sixteen, Father Laport was hit in the thigh during a basketball game in South Boston. The bruise got progressively larger, and within a year he died from leukemia. Everyone who knew him was greatly saddened by his death. (Several years after Father Laport's death, the residents of South Boston built a beautiful statue of him right across from the "L" Street Lockers, a focal point of their community. Every Saint Patrick's Day the parade stops in front of his statue to remember and honor him.)

I decided to join the priesthood both because it provided a lot of social status within my world and also, due to Father Laport's example, I wanted to make a positive difference in other people's lives. I decided to attend the Maryknoll Seminary in Glen Ellen,

Illinois, a missionary society known as the "Marines" of the American Catholic Church. Seminary life consisted of prayer, study and work. I can still remember the power of 300 men sitting in a beautiful circular green marble chapel, singing vespers. I connected most with an older Benedictine from France. As a young priest he threw an SS trooper out of a window in order to protect Jewish people who lived in his town. He then fled to North Africa and somehow ended up teaching French outside of Chicago. He had such a loving presence that I loved to serve as his altar boy whenever he celebrated Mass.

I entered the seminary believing totally in what the Church taught, which included believing totally in the Bible. During one of my first scripture courses I learned that the Book of Genesis was made up of various creation stories from other religious traditions. I was astonished. If Genesis was not literally true, then what else had I been told that wasn't true? Shocked by this discovery and resentful that I had been lied to for so many years, I lost my faith. Also, the advertisements for women's lingerie in the *New York Times* Sunday magazine sections were starting to look awfully good to me. I left the seminary. I also gave up on Roman Catholicism and for years thereafter searched for truth by attending a wide variety of different churches.

In 1967 I graduated from Duquesne University in Pittsburgh with a major in Political Science. Just before getting my diploma I received a draft notice from the Army. This was during the height of the Tet Offensive in Vietnam. Several years earlier I had an industrial accident during a summer job. I was working in a tanning company in Haverhill, and the foreman told me to clean a large machine that had two huge rollers through which hides traveled, like a huge old washing machine with two wringers to take excess water out of the clothes. My hand was wrapped inside a cleaning rag when all of a sudden the tip of the rag got caught between the rollers and pulled my arm into the machine. There was no one in the room and the only switch to stop the machine was on a far wall. As I screamed, people rushed in. They had to take the machine apart in order to free my arm. The rollers had peeled off my skin and muscle right down to the bone. Not only could I see my bone, but the whole right side of my body was covered with blood since all the vessels in my arm had been severed. Realizing that I was bleeding to death, I used what I had learned as an Eagle Scout, took a rag and a wrench and put a tourniquet on my forearm while waiting for the ambulance to come.

At the local hospital they were preparing the operating room to amputate my arm. My parents insisted that I be taken to Massachusetts General Hospital in Boston where my arm was repaired by the same surgical team which a few months earlier had been the first in history to replace a limb. After an eight–hour operation and two months in the hospital, my arm was healed and functioning and I returned to college. Ironically, this accident was fortunate because if I had gone to Vietnam with the attitude I had then, I would have ended up either a drug addict or dead.

Achieving the American Dream

During my senior year in college I hitched a ride with a salesman whose description of his work impressed me so much that I decided that instead of being a lawyer, I too would go into sales.

After graduating from college I began my business career selling for major medical corporations. I loved strategizing and then interacting with people to implement my sales plans, and quickly became one of the top sales producers in whichever company I was working. I helped bring the Boston pharmaceutical division of

Pfizer from the lowest to number one in the country and was awarded for being one of the top ten sales producers in the United States for Johnson & Johnson. Even though I was still seeking truth by attending many different churches, none of them gave me the answers I was looking for. Increasingly, the external world of material achievement became the only reality that mattered to me, and I became extremely successful.

By 1980, at the age of 35, I had achieved what most people would consider the "American Dream." I was at the top income level of my profession; had a wife and a daughter; owned a large new custom–built house, a 30–foot sailboat, and two new cars. Yet inside I felt a deep emptiness. Looking back, I now realize that I used competition, material objects, achievement, and a total emphasis on performance to compensate for a deep sense of unhappiness and an almost nonexistent self–esteem. I can see now that I was extremely selfish and self–centered, with a "put myself first" attitude, using anyone and anything in an attempt to satisfy my inner needs. But success provided only a short–lived sense of satisfaction. There had to be more to life than just satisfying my egotistical needs, but I did not know what it was.

One morning while I was shaving, I heard a voice telling me to write a book. For someone with no inner life this was a big surprise. I had no desire to write a book and no idea what to write about.

The real beginning of my personal journey of discovery also began in 1980, when I had just separated from my wife and left our house. I felt like an absolute failure. Since I had promised a business colleague that I would attend an Amway conference, I attended alone. Amway conventions are filled with husbands and wives working together, an environment which rubbed salt into my wound. After the convention, as I was driving to my motel, I cried out to God from the bottom of my soul—"Why?"

In my motel room I noticed a small brochure which described Norman Vincent Peale's new book, *The Positive Power of Jesus Christ*. The brief description seemed an answer to my cry. On returning to Boston I searched through numerous bookstores for Peale's book, but none of them had it in stock. Later that month, as I was working the Maine territory, I noticed a bookstore in a small mall near my hotel. They had Dr. Peale's book. Back in my hotel room I eagerly began to read it, and after about 20 pages I suddenly had what I learned later was a mystical experience. The room seemed to fill with a smoky mist. I grabbed a piece of paper from the desk and wrote:

April 15, 1980   Augusta, Maine

I, Jack Beauregard, will follow a new path in my life. Anything that is an obstacle will be eliminated. My life from this point on is to love and share this love with all people who are searching . . .

Five months later at a private singles club in Boston, I met Judy Ahrens, a flight attendant with Eastern Airlines. We were attracted to each other and began dating. After a few weeks she told me that on April 15—the same night that I had my mystical experience—she heard a voice she did not recognize calling her name. She knew then that she had to make deep changes in her life. We both realized we had met a soulmate for the first time in our lives and we married.

Judy and I had a lot of fun together. On our vacations we drank wines at chateaus in Bordeaux and in vineyards in the Rhine Valley, drove from the Loire Valley to the Alps, walked some of the world's most beautiful beaches, made from the whitest to the blackest sand. When we sailed in the Caribbean, we marveled at the darkest night skies, which were filled with the sequins of thousands of stars. Judy continued her career as a flight attendant, and I continued to work as a top salesman in the medical products industry.

As a salesman your car is your office, and the ultimate car at that time was a Mercedes–Benz. In 1982 I was in a hotel room in Stuttgart, Germany, with Judy and my teenage daughter Amy. We were preparing to pick up my new Mercedes–Benz the next morning and achieve my ultimate dream. During the night I was suddenly awakened by a clear voice. I sat bolt upright in bed and heard this voice tell me to apply the talents I had used for material success and go inward. I saw no one in the room, and both Judy and Amy were fast asleep. I was totally astonished and wondered what in the world was going on. Then somehow I fell back asleep.

The next morning I told Judy and Amy about the voice that I had heard. Although I did not know exactly what it meant, we all understood that something new had now started in my life and I would pursue it to the end.

Beginning the Inner Journey

Upon returning to the United States, my life did not change immediately. Continuing in my path of material success, I became national salesman of the year for the biomedical division of C.R. Bard. After declining to be their West Coast sales manager, I entered the world of the entrepreneur, becoming a commissioned salesman with Zimmer, the largest orthopedic company in the world. I was now at the top of my field. I often stood right in the operating room, telling the surgeon the techniques for implementing our total hip or knee replacements. (In fact, one of my colleagues actually performed surgery, because he knew the most effective way to implement the total hip replacement that he sold. The State of New York happened to be doing an accreditation in this hospital at the same time, and this incident was picked up by the media and became the material for a book titled *Salesman/Surgeon.*)

After the government implemented a test program in cost–containment in the state of New Jersey, I realized that cost–containment was going to become a reality. I developed a marketing plan, contacted suppliers in the Midwest and throughout Germany, and began the first company in the U.S. to offer orthopedic trauma implants and surgical instruments at a 30% discount. I sold a quarter of a million dollars of company shares to surgeon investors. My company, Designer Orthopedics, also created custom–made surgical instruments for surgeons. Our innovative products included a patented bone biopsy needle and a series of spinal instruments that were later used in surgery on Larry Bird's back. I brought the company from no sales to a multimillion dollar venture with 120 commissioned salespeople in 42 states. While building my company, I finally began to explore and develop a new model for living.

When I first met Judy, I did not know what to make of her, because the way she thought was so much larger than anything I had ever encountered. Even though I was very attracted to her, I found her quite intimidating at first because I could not pigeonhole her into any of my existing mental categories. While Judy and I were getting to know each other, a new series was being aired on PBS–TV, "Cosmos" with Carl Sagan. After watching the first program I knew that "Cosmos" was going to be critical with regard to where our relationship was going. I would either stay within my familiar belief systems or allow my mind to stretch in unexpected new directions. Week by week, as we watched the programs, I opened up more and more to the wisdom and beauty of the universe, gradually coming to realize that what I was watching on TV was the handiwork of the God to whom I had always prayed. By the end of the series I felt a sense of awe that I was able to understand some fundamental aspects of the creative force which permeates the universe. I will never forget the statement that ended "Cosmos":

> We are the local embodiments of a Cosmos grown to self–awareness. We have begun to contemplate our origins: starstuff pondering the stars; organized assemblages of ten billion billion billion atoms considering the evolution of atoms; tracing the long journey by which, here at last, consciousness arose. Our loyalties are to the species and the planet. We speak for Earth. Our obligation to survive is owed not just to ourselves but also to that Cosmos, ancient and vast, from which we spring.[2]

A part of me had always been struggling to find something greater in life, especially when I realized that the way I was living was not working. I had tried to find answers in making money, in corporate promotion, in owning status possessions, or trying to get high through addictions. I realized that I was living my life in my head because I was disconnected from my feelings, and that even though I was highly "religious," I had no inner spiritual life. I needed to create a balance between my external life and an inner life, as the clear message that I had received in Stuttgart told me.

By acknowledging my spiritual connection to the larger cosmos and discovering that science was developing a new perspective which accepted and even supported a spiritual view of the universe, I felt that I had broken through to a new paradigm which could provide me with a better basis for living. Now I would have to learn more about this new model, so I could integrate and apply it to my everyday life.

Between 1982 and 1985, in addition to my duties as a corporate president, I was also a Special Student at Harvard Divinity School, taking graduate course in Comparative Religious Studies. My goal was to study the effects of belief systems on our personal lives, and to be able to use all of Harvard's libraries for research for this book.

I began to read books on subjects I had never thought about before, including psychology, mythology, spiritual traditions from around the world, and also continued to learn about the latest discoveries from physics and other scientific disciplines.

Another reason I went to Harvard Divinity School was because my life was spiritually unfulfilled. All the churches I attended revolved around externals: attending Mass, reading the Bible, singing hymns, listening to sermons, or receiving the Eucharist, and none of this satisfied me. I wanted to open myself to other spiritual traditions, to learn how other people around the world and through the centuries approached spirituality.

I discovered that both Buddhism and certain traditions in Hinduism have focused not on trying to understand the nature of physical reality, as Westerners do, but on discovering the most effective way to contact the Infinite. I liked the concept that a person can experience his inner divinity directly. I also discovered that a mystical tradition existed in the West, in which men and women throughout the centuries wrote about their direct experiences of personal contact with God. I realized I was searching for spiritual answers, and that these mystical traditions spoke to my spiritual longings.

During these years I also discovered that both quantum physics and the mystical explanation of reality are almost identical. And I was inspired by attending one of the first Mind/Body conferences held in Boston, where medical professionals presented research about the inherent interconnectedness of our bodies and minds, and even spoke about after–life experiences. What I saw emerging was not wishful New Age thinking, but a new scientific paradigm created from assumptions and beliefs totally different from the ones that most of us were taught. The latest scientific discoveries from the new science, regarding the interconnectedness, oneness, and wholeness of physical reality, were especially appealing to me, since all my life I had felt separated and isolated from others.

During this time Judy told me that she wanted some help in her personal work. One day at divinity school I noticed a flyer on the bulletin board about the "Opening Your Heart Workshop." I told Judy about it and she joined the workshop, which consisted of a weekly group meeting, weekly individual sessions with a counselor, weekly meetings with a partner from the group, and an intense weekend during each six–month period. I am grateful that I joined this workshop too. If I hadn't, Judy would have grown and I would have stayed stuck at the same level of personal development. I give my parents credit for joining me at one session, where my mother gave me permission to become more loving and accepting like my father. After two and a half years of this personal transformation work, both Judy and I graduated from the group. Shortly after that Judy gave birth to our son Justin.

While I was attending Harvard Divinity School and the "Opening Your Heart Workshop," I began to discover that so many of my unconscious assumptions, beliefs, and images were negative. I realized that trying to live only in the positive was unnatural because everything and everyone has both a positive and negative aspect, and denying my negatives actually allowed negativity to continue its hold over my life. The only way I could make real, meaningful changes was to first become aware of the unconscious negative beliefs and images I had about myself, remember all the hurtful things that I had done to other people, and all the times that I had been hurt, which I had repressed and denied. Only then could I begin to create genuine positive alternatives in my life.

My life slowly began to change. What I had formerly thought were big life concerns now began to seem small and unimportant, while what I had thought was trivial became important. I continued to work on psychological issues which I had previously ignored, focusing on obstacles which had been blocking my personal growth. As the various principles and insights from psychology, cosmology, spirituality, and my own inner work began to operate in my life, I slowly stopped being so hard on myself, realizing that I was only human and there was no such thing as perfection. I began to realize that my emphasis on always being "right" made my life rigid and mechanical, preventing me from being natural and enjoying what I was doing. At some point I became aware that a sense of humor is a sign of spontaneity and creativity and I began to laugh at my mistakes. For example, when I dropped something I could now laugh, telling people that I was just checking to see if gravity still works, since there might be some place on this planet where instead of things falling to the ground, they might fly up.

I began to be less envious of other people's good fortune and stopped wishing that I were someone else. As my self–confidence increased, I became less anxious and insecure. This allowed me to stop being jealous, and resulted in many fewer arguments and fights. I actually started to like myself and gradually, very gradually, I even began to love myself.

As I continued to share my discoveries with Judy, I realized that I was becoming open to and working out of a new paradigm, which integrated spirituality, personal growth, and the new science. I began to refer to this new paradigm as the "Balanced Paradigm," since it balanced the inner and the outer, the scientific and the spiritual. Increasingly I discovered evidence for this new paradigm all around me, which resulted in a positive feedback system, since the more I opened my mind the more evidence I found, and the more my mind continued to open. Excited about these discoveries, Judy and I formed "Innervisions," a company which would teach this new perspective to others.

In 1987 we learned that Judy had breast cancer. After several months of treatment she was given a clean bill of health and went back to work. Unknown to us, the cancer had metastasized. A few months later she discovered a lump in her stomach and was diagnosed with liver cancer.

I will never forget the day Judy's oncologist called. I answered the phone, and he told me that the cancer in her liver was inoperable and there were no more chemotherapy regimens available. Stunned, I asked him how long she had to live, and he said, "four weeks." In shock I gave the phone to Judy, and as he gave her the death sentence, I tried to figure out what to say to my best friend, the person I most loved and the mother of our young son, when she was hearing that she had only four weeks to live.

As she hung up the phone, words failed me. Then I felt words emerging from the deepest part of my being and I told her, "Sit down. You have only four weeks to live. The question is, how do you want to spend these last four weeks? You can use your remaining time positively or negatively. The choice is yours."

Judy chose the positive even in the face of terminal cancer. Her courage had a major impact on many, many lives since her attitude reflected her philosophy that without courageous love there is no freedom. She created the ultimate freedom in choosing how she was going to die.

As soon as we heard that diagnosis, I called an emergency Board of Directors meeting to discuss the future of Designer Orthopedics. I informed the board members that I was no longer able to run the company, travel around the country, and at the same time take care of my wife as she went through the process of dying, and also care for our two–year–old son, Justin. All the common shares of the company had been sold and I was in the process of selling a new issue of preferred shares for $350,000 to help finance the company.

When the board members decided that they would not invest the needed $350,000 capital, I realized that my life's focus on success and achievement had suddenly and completely been taken away from me.

The night she went into the hospital to die, Judy wrote me a note which said, "The world needs what you have. You might not have all the answers, but you can help all those who are searching." I made her a vow, not how or where to bring up our son, but that I would write this book. Judy even made sure that I worked on the book when I was with her on the cancer ward in the hospital. Since by that time I had developed the concept of the Balanced Paradigm and the Power of Balance process, I finally knew what this book was going to be about.

After Judy died, I became "Mr. Mom" for Justin. (I was his primary caretaker from age two until he was nine, when I married Maureen.) I was able to stay home with Justin during his early years. When he took naps and at night, I continued doing research for and writing this book.

Moving from "Before Transformation" to "After Transformation"

Transformation is a fact of life. Everything in the universe has a tendency to move toward fulfillment of its inner nature, and that also applies to you and me. For example, the seed of an apple contains the potential of its roots, trunk, twigs, branches, leaves, and fruits, and it will do whatever it can to bring that inner potential into reality. Your courage in seeking a life of deeper fulfillment and meaning also reflects this universal tendency towards transformation. The Power of Balance has had such a powerful effect on my life that I now describe my life as " B.T." (before transformation), and "A.T." (after transformation). I cannot tell you that on a certain day something profound happened to me, because personal transformation is very much like a series of small snowstorms in winter. At some point you notice that the snow has accumulated—something very different has now come into existence.

Figure 1.1. summarizes my key beliefs B.T., and how they changed, A. T. You can see how my beliefs B.T. reflect two major cultural paradigms which influence many of us: traditional religion and our modern secular culture. My childhood upbringing and religion, which taught me that we were created by a harsh, distant, judgmental, authoritarian God, led to my need to appear "perfect" and to my constant feelings of separateness and isolation. And the larger culture's emphasis on individual achievement and material affluence led to my need to dominate and control others, and to my overemphasis on achieving material success as a substitute for inner fulfillment, balance, and authentic spirituality.

You could describe my personal process of transformation by saying that I gradually went through a "paradigm shift." A paradigm refers to a larger worldview or understanding of reality, usually shared by many people. Although I went through a personal paradigm shift as step–by–step I dramatically transformed my own beliefs, attitudes, and actions, my journey was also part of a larger cultural paradigm shift now taking place.

Even though my personal transformation—from "B.T." to "A.T."—came out of my personal history, background, upbringing, life experiences, unique personality, and plenty of hard work, it's also obvious that my beliefs and values B.T. were shaped by larger cultural beliefs, which came from my parents, teachers, religion, the media, etc. Furthermore, the new ideas in psychology, science, and spirituality

The Author's Key Beliefs
"Before Transformation" and "After Transformation"

Before Transformation (B.T.)	After Transformation (A.T.)
1. Materialism. Only material success counts.	**1. We are spiritual beings.** Actually, we are both material and spiritual, and need to recognize both aspects of life.
2. False Self: I am always right. Other people are to blame for the negative things that happen to me.	**2. I am in process.** I contain both positive and negative aspects. I take responsibility for my actions, accepting my negatives and transforming them into positives.
3. Polarized (Dominator) thinking. The world is made up of distinct opposites. Everything is either/or. You are either a winner or a loser.	**3. Seeming opposites are actually in dynamic balance, interconnected aspects of a dynamic whole.** I can integrate my own apparent opposites: head/heart; intellect/emotions; masculinity/femininity, etc. I have many more choices than merely "either/or."

4. Isolation. I am separate from the universe. I am separate from the divine. I am separate from other people, and care only about myself.	**4. Everything is connected**. The universe is alive, and I am part of and co–creator with the universe. The creator is in creation, and I too, am an expression of the Divine Creative Force. I can connect to other people through love. My actions (and the actions of each of us) can help bring more love and balance into the world.
5. Control. To achieve my goals, I need to control the people and events around me.	**5. I can let go and trust the process.** By opening to the intelligence of the universe, I allow what I need (both lessons and "miracles") to come to me.

Figure 1.1.

which helped me go through my transformation were available to me because they are part of a new worldview which is now emerging at the end of the 20th century.[3]

My personal transformation demonstrates that each of us is not only shaped by the larger cultural worldview and era in which we live, but each of us is also a co–creator of our larger world, with our own unique gifts, mission, and destiny. Because all reality is interconnected, changing yourself as an individual can influence the larger world; each of us can indeed make a difference. *It's selfish not to do personal work.*

Sharing the Power of Balance with Others

Now that I have done so much personal work, and am living so much more truly as the person I was meant to be, my passion is to share this process of transformation and the transformational worldview behind it with others.

Writing this book is of course one key way to share this message. Because of my extensive experience in business, I can also see numerous implications for applying the principles of the Power of Balance beyond personal transformation, to organizations. During the past few years I have been presenting seminars and workshops about the Balanced Paradigm and the Power of Balance especially as they apply to transform business organizations for success in the 21st century, and will continue to do so. I also plan to write more about how the Power of Balance process can be applied to our society.

Several people who have known me through my life and work, and watched as I went through the process of transformation, have written about what they observed. Since their observations provide a balanced perspective to my own, I would like to share some of their comments with you.

First is a letter from a psychiatrist who was a business associate for many years:

Jack doesn't look the role of prophet or visionary. In fact, descriptive adjectives only offer a picture of contradictions. He wears suits with white shirts and conservative ties. He's kind of a faded guru and worn warrior....The strength of his words, the power of his conviction, the depth of his feelings, the gravity of the ideas, yet the soft, gentle wisdom of his delivery made me sit up and take notice. The argument of walking the talk comes to mind. Jack walks the talk....

Next is a letter from the head of training and development at a local hospital where I gave one of my workshops:

I first met Jack in 1987. He called to talk to me about presenting a continuing education program about a new paradigm. As health care was in the midst of rapid change, I was interested in meeting with him to discuss this further. As Jack presented his theory, I became more and more fascinated with this new Balanced Paradigm, so I contracted with him to do a program for the nurses to demonstrate how this philosophy would fit into their everyday lives and their nursing care.

The evening of the program, Jack arrived and quietly announced to me that his wife had been diagnosed with breast cancer earlier in the day. I could not believe that he had not canceled. As I displayed my shock at his insistence to go on with the program, he simply stated that he and his wife had decided that now more than ever they must continue in the practice of their beliefs or all the years of researching and developing his theory would be for naught. That night, Jack won my respect and my heart. Life and death followed for Jack, and the raising of his son Justin by himself became a remarkable thing to watch. The operationalizing of Jack's beliefs in a balanced existence and changing the negative to the positive, seemed to empower Justin to be loving and trusting. The literature certainly reflects the negatives of losing one's mother at an early age. At this writing, Jack's son has not displayed any of them.

As I watched this man raising a toddler alone, adjusting to his profound loss, and diligently working to get out his message, I felt the time had come. The book had to be written now! I strongly urged him to begin the first book, because he was already living book two or three.

Bill Scherkenbach at General Motors defines a theory as a 'special combination of inputs that derives from the past and affects the future.' I feel this Balanced Paradigm, Jack's profound reflections on the universe's and man's past, and his interpretation of its meaning in the present, will definitely affect the future.

There is no belief or paradigm that will take away the pain of life or the negative experiences that day to day living brings. But the paradigm that Jack proposes will help to see life and death as a continuum of experiences and resources that fit into the overall cosmic plan; and that life can be best managed by acknowledgment and acceptance of one's singular life in relationship to this overall plan.

As the writer of that letter observed, I used the principles of the Power of Balance to transform the way I raised Justin. I made sure that he never lost connection with his own heart and soul, and I never conditioned him to believe that his basic nature was sinful. Therefore, he never internalized the false idea that his life was a mistake of creation. He was taught both to be centered and to be open to the full range of options in life. Today, at the age of 15 he is incredibly aware and compassionate, with an amazing ability to be poised and to make connections at a deep level with the people he meets. In fact, he is the most loving child I have ever met. You may think I am biased, because he's my son—so don't take my word for it. His teachers' comments on his school report cards constantly describe him as helpful and caring to his classmates, as being centered, a peacemaker, and a role model. In fact, as I was writing this section, I received Justin's year–end report card, on which his fifth–grade teacher had written:

> Justin, I'm really going to miss you! *NEVER* have I taught anyone so thoughtful, so considerate, so freely helpful as you! I will always remember this special class and above all, you! Remember our year together with fondness. And my very best wishes for a safe, fun–filled summer and a wonderful 6th grade experience! There was an additional handwritten note on the outside folder, which said: To one boy who's holding a VERY special place in my heart. I love you, Justin.

Chapter 2

Four Keys to Self–Transformation

As I participated in the process of personal transformation, I discovered four fundamental insights which guided me throughout this work. (See Figure 2.1.)

Four Keys to Self–Transformation

1. What you believe creates your reality.

   Change your beliefs and you change your world.

2. Understanding alone is not enough.

   You must also act on your new understandings.

3. Change takes time.

4. You can trust the process.

   The universe supports your transformation.

Figure 2.1.

Changing Your Beliefs, Changing Your Reality

A major key to self–transformation is understanding how powerfully our beliefs shape our reality, and realizing that as we change our belief systems, we can change our experiences, our lives, even our world.

If we believe something is possible, we will try to achieve it. On the other hand, if we believe something is not possible, then we will not bother trying to make it happen. In both positive and negative ways, our belief systems create our models of the world and what we think is possible in it, defining who we are and what we perceive as reality.

Many great thinkers and traditions emphasize the importance of belief systems. The Bible states that "Whatever a man thinks, so is he." The Indian *Bhagavad Gita* says that "Man is made by his beliefs. As he believes, so he is." The Buddha said in the *Dhammapada*, "We are what we think. All that we are arises with our thoughts. With our thoughts we make our world." Marcus Aurelius wrote, "Your life is what your thoughts make it." And Shakespeare suggested, "There is nothing good or bad, but thinking makes it so." William James, the famous American psychologist, stated that "The great discovery of my generation is that men can alter their lives by altering their attitudes in their minds."And Dr. Walter Scott, President of Northwestern University wrote that "Success or failure is caused by mental attitudes even more than by mental capacities."

The concept that our beliefs create our reality is well known today, not just in "New Age" circles but also in psychology, medicine, even in business and sales training, and many books and seminars are devoted to teaching how to apply this concept for personal empowerment, growth, or business success. Our mental beliefs can actually create our personal physical reality, as I learned from the following examples given at a conference on mind/body medicine.

During a football game in Monterey Park, California, officials announced over the public address system that the soda being sold at a concession stand had been poisoned. Upon hearing this announcement many people in the stands suddenly became seriously ill. Ambulances had to shuttle fainting and vomiting people to six area hospitals. Soon thereafter a doctor determined that the original person's illness was due to a bottle of soda from one faulty soda machine. When this information was announced over the public address system the sudden, mass illness that had fallen upon the spectators immediately stopped.

In another example, 150 medical students were given various psychotropic drugs. Half of the students were told they were receiving a tranquilizer, while the other half were told they were receiving an antidepressant. In actuality the two medications were switched, so that the group who thought they were getting the tranquilizer actually received the antidepressant, and the group who thought they were getting the antidepressant actually received the tranquilizer. In more than 50 percent of the cases, the students showed symptoms which reflected what they *thought* they had been given! For these students, their power of belief was so strong that it not only overcame the effect of the active ingredients in the medications; it actually created different physical symptoms, which matched the subject's assumptions and beliefs. This is just one more demonstration that what we believe can create the "reality" which we actually experience in everyday life.

At a sales training meeting, I saw a video which dramatically demonstrated how our beliefs can create limiting "mental walls" which restrict our actions. A large fish—a Northern pike—was placed in a spacious fish tank, then a smaller fish tank was inverted and put over the pike. Smaller fish, its natural food, were then placed in the water just outside the inverted tank. Every time that pike went to feed on the smaller fish, it would hit the glass walls of the inverted tank. The more it kept trying, the more it would hit those walls. After a while the smaller tank was removed, so that the pike could now swim out to catch its prey—but that pike stayed within the confines of the now removed barrier. It believed that those walls were still there, even though they were now gone. That pike was starving, and its food was swimming all around it, but it couldn't move out beyond its self–imposed walls to get what it needed.

I had created limiting mental walls in my own life, through my beliefs that "I can't do that" or "This is impossible." In order to achieve my own transformation, I first had to balance these limiting assumptions by creating positive alternatives and beliefs. As I describe in the next chapter, when I brought my limiting beliefs to light and created new, expanded mental options, I eventually changed my emotions, my body, my relationships, and my spiritual consciousness.

Awareness—Acceptance—Action as Keys to Self–Transformation

Following the direction of the voice I heard in Stuttgart, I used the pragmatic skills which had brought me external success, and applied them to the discoveries I made on my inner journey. This helped me realize that while expanded awareness is essential to transforming one's life, it must also be balanced with effective action in order to make meaningful changes. From this realization I developed a three–step process, which I call "Awareness—Acceptance—Action." This was a powerful tool which allowed me to move from inner realization to outer manifestation as I applied it in every step of my personal transformation work.

Step 1. Awareness

Expanding one's awareness far beyond the confines of one's limiting assumptions, beliefs, and convictions frees up a tremendous amount of energy, and is the first step toward becoming whole. When our awareness is limited, things happen to us and we don't know why. We may believe we are in control, but in actuality we are ruled by our unconscious beliefs and assumptions, often to our detriment.

Machinery runs automatically, that is, without awareness, and even though we are human, many of us live day–to–day on automatic pilot. It's no coincidence that Webster's Dictionary defines "automatic" as "done without conscious thought or volition, as if *mechanically*." The alternative is to become more mindful or aware. John R. Grinnell, Jr. defines awareness as "the ability to stand outside a system to view it, thereby understanding the system..."[4] In this case, the system is your inner being. Or as Socrates taught many centuries ago, "Know Thyself."

As I explain in detail in the next chapter, becoming aware of one's Shadow, with all its unattractive, negative contents, can be an extremely emotional and upsetting experience at first. As you face your Shadow you might become filled with anger, shame, guilt, revulsion, self–condemnation, or a whole host of other negative feelings toward yourself. Or you might find yourself blaming the contents and actions of your Shadow on the people who brought you up—for example, on abusive or rejecting parents, or other caretakers and authority figures from your past.

While such reactions, either toward yourself or others are entirely understandable, they must also be transcended in order for you to become whole. There is no point in denying that your parents and other caretakers did whatever they did; and perhaps this is part of the reason for your Shadow. Nevertheless, if you get stuck in anger, blaming, and other such emotions either toward yourself or others, you are still getting trapped by negativity.

Step 2. Acceptance.

As Ralph Waldo Emerson said, "Trust Thyself." Accepting yourself is not denial. You are not denying the reality of who you are, what you have done to others, or what happened to you. Instead, you simply *accept* who you are and what happened, as part of your past. And then you let any negative feelings go. If you feel that others were responsible for your bad behavior, accept that those people did the best they knew how, and (hopefully) it was not their intention to be malicious. They were simply acting as *they* were taught, in reaction to how their experiences influenced them.

Forgiving yourself and others is an important part of acceptance. Forgiveness promotes self–cleansing of negativity by allowing you to let go of your resentments, shame, or feelings of guilt and inferiority. As you release negativity, you create emotional and energetic space to move into the next step.

Step 3. Action

After you become more fully aware of yourself, in both your positive and negative aspects, and let go of blame toward yourself by accepting who you really are, you are now ready to participate actively in your process of growth. Or as Kierkegaard said, "Choose Thyself."

The fact is that no one but you can do what you need to do in order to transform your life. The positive side is that by opening your mind and life to new possibilities and taking responsibility for your destiny, you will feel a sense of empowerment. Active participation in reconstructing yourself and redirecting your life creates a sense of confidence and leads to the success and satisfaction of having made meaningful changes in your life.

Participating in the process of Awareness–Acceptance–Action has brought me many benefits. Perhaps most significant, it has enabled me to stop blaming others, and to take responsibility for my own attitudes, emotions, actions, and reactions. By becoming able to accept my negative emotions and reactions as a natural part of my emotional spectrum, I gradually became able to recognize when other people were "pushing my buttons" and causing my "old tapes" to be played. This allowed me to realize that no one else can make me feel a certain way, since this power is only within me.

As I began to take responsibility for my feelings, my relationships with other people began to change for the better, since I now realized that my negative emotions were *my* issues, not theirs.

Change Takes Time

I found that in order to make meaningful, transformational change, I had to let go of my impatience. Like most of us, I was part of the "credit card generation." I wanted things now. I was not used to waiting. But this does not work when you are making changes for a lifetime. Anything worthwhile is worth working for and takes time, and this is especially true for your life.

As I continued with my transformation process, I learned that generally it does not happen instantaneously. Transformation evolves in your life by degrees. Picture yourself walking up a flight of stairs in a tall building. In order to get to the top you have to climb flight after flight of stairs. In the same way, in order to reach your true self and begin to live a more meaningful life, you also need to spend the time and effort to evolve to each new level of transformation.

The Universe Supports Transformation

The mechanistic or Newtonian view of the universe describes a rigidly structured world made up of material objects such as the planets or our own bodies, which change when they are influenced by physical forces like gravity and inertia. By contrast, the "new science" is discovering that we live in a dynamic universe, characterized by numerous coherent systems—be they galaxies, planets, bacteria, plants, animals, human beings, etc.—each of which is in the process of changing and being transformed. We are now learning that the universe is designed to promote evolution, that the universe is in effect a *process* of change, with new order arising out of chaos; and we can participate consciously in this natural process. In Chapter 4, I describe in more detail the new scientific discoveries which can help us trust the process of our own self–transformation, because we understand that transformation is an inherent aspect of the universe.

Before Transformation, when I used to live in fear and insecurity, I had a constant need for power and control. Now I am genuinely able to trust that whatever happens to me in the long term is best. I have learned that I was created by and am part of the energy and matter of the universe. The universe is inside my body, its spirit and intelligence are inside my center, so why not trust? B.T., I was constantly fighting to swim upstream, until I realized that downstream is the direction in which the river of evolution naturally flows. I stopped struggling, lay down and floated in the water, and now feel carried along by the river as it moves to merge into the sea. At the end of this journey is a larger world of true fulfillment and meaning.

This new concept of the universe as dynamic process can reinforce our efforts to expand our beliefs and assumptions. The only thing that holds us in our present "tank" is our current thinking. We need to take a chance and swim out of the tank of our current models and mindsets. The potential of changing our minds, and thereby changing reality, affects us not only at the individual level, but also beyond. We can create a paradigm shift by remolding and expanding what we think is possible. When enough of us change our minds, the world will change.

Chapter 3

Going Within: Reclaiming the Shadow

Acknowledging the False Self

The first step toward my personal transformation was realizing that I had created and identified with a False Self, which prevented me from connecting and living with my authentic inner self. This False Self presented me with the illusionary image that I was always right, and therefore there was no need for me to change. If anything bad happened to me it was always someone else's fault. While this False Self reassured me that I could do no wrong, I was always blaming others for the many things that did go wrong.

I further discovered that this False Self was keeping me separated from a hidden part of myself—a part which many psychologists and spiritual seekers call the "Shadow." My unrecognized Shadow was holding all my repressed pain and disappointments, and all the mean, selfish acts I had done to others—everything my illusionary "perfect" self wanted to forget. Yet while I denied my Shadow, I constantly projected these hidden, undesirable parts of myself onto the people and world around me. In fact, these hidden negative aspects of myself actually controlled my life and prevented me from achieving true fulfillment and self–love.

Negativity was an extremely large part of my Shadow. My working definition of negativity includes: extremely limiting, closed beliefs; a lack of psychological essentials such as feelings of self–esteem, value, and self–worth; a fearful, anxious emotional response to life and a tendency toward self–defensive behaviors.

Because my False Self denied the existence of my many negative beliefs and actions, I lived for many years under the illusion that I was strong, positive, and in control. In reality I lacked the most basic positive characteristics, such as an open approach to life, a predisposition to love, and a willingness to do whatever needs to be done to facilitate my personal growth and success, starting with taking responsibility for my Shadow.

The Shadow: A Key to Wholeness

A fictional analogy of doing your Shadow work is the scene in which Tinker Bell and Peter Pan are looking for Peter's missing shadow in the nursery. When you reattach your Shadow, as Wendy did for Peter, it might hurt a little at first but it will make you whole. The Shadow is actually a complementary "dark side" that makes up our whole personality. Or as the eminent psychologist Carl Jung wrote, "One does not become enlightened by imagining figures of light, but by making the darkness conscious."

A real world analogy for the Shadow is the moon. The moon is always whole, even though we usually see only its lighted portion. The moon's other half—its dark side—is still there. You can see the whole moon only when its surface is totally lighted, during a full moon, or when it is totally dark, during a lunar eclipse. Light and shadow are complementary opposites. Stand in the light and you will see your shadow.

Another analogy for our Shadow is a tree. When you look at a tree you see its trunk and branches, yet the tree stands because it also has roots hidden in the ground. By denying that my Shadow existed, I denied half of who I was, which meant I could not experience wholeness and completeness. In order to become whole again, I needed to become aware of the negative assumptions, beliefs, emotions, and experiences that had been repressed and stored in my Shadow.

Doing my Shadow work was like going down into a mine shaft. Although it was dark and I became aware of ever deeper darkness, paradoxically a bright light began to appear the deeper I descended. At the bottom of the mine I found my true center, my original inner core. According to Carl Jung:

> When an individual makes an attempt to see his Shadow, he becomes aware of and is often ashamed of, those qualities and impulses he denies in himself, but can plainly see in other people, such as egotism, mental laziness, sloppiness, unreal fantasies, schemes and plots, carelessness, and cowardice, inordinate love of money and possessions, in short all the little sins about which he might previously have told himself that 'it doesn't matter.' Nobody will notice it and in any case other people do it too.[5]

After having spent many years doing my Shadow work, I accept the fact that the negatives which I was conditioned into will always be there. They are permanent grooves, like a record in my mind. Despite the preaching of the "Gospel of Positive Thinking," I cannot simply wish my negatives away. I was only able to make meaningful, permanent changes in my life by first acknowledging, rather than denying, my Shadow. Before Transformation (B.T.) I often read self–help books, agreed with what they were saying, yet never really made the positive changes that they presented. In fact, I would actually feel worse after reading them. The "Gospel of Positive Thinking" did not work because denying my negatives only enabled them to grow stronger. Only by becoming aware of and accepting my hidden negatives was I finally freed from their grip.

The Nature of the Shadow

In the prevailing cultural paradigms, a high value is placed on the positive aspects of life by denying the existence of one's negative characteristics. This imbalanced focus on the positive has been passed down from generation to generation resulting in cultural denial which has contributed to the creation of our Shadows. This imbalanced focus on the positive at the expense of the negative is reflected in the way many of us were raised. Our childhood experiences often influenced us to split off parts of ourselves that were not appreciated by our caretakers. Many of us were taught to repress whatever issues our parents considered "negative," such as their own negative characteristics, that they were conditioned to suppress, or issues that they had failed to work out in their own lives. For example, you may have been told: "I never want to hear you say that again" or "We don't act like that in this family." My religious conditioning also contributed to the creation of my Shadow because it taught me to believe that I was sinful if I had negative thoughts, regardless of whether or not I acted on them. I discovered that my Shadow was responsible for the development of my False Self at the expense of living from my authentic self. Whatever did not fit into my ideal image of myself was a direct threat to the false positive self–image of my False Self, so I buried these parts in my unconscious.

Not only were we taught to repress the unacceptable parts of ourselves, we were also conditioned not to appreciate our innate talents. As I did my Shadow work, I not only discovered repressed negative aspects of myself, but also natural talents that had been repressed in my life for years.

In my inward journey I discovered two basic functions of the Shadow. It both concealed the negatives in my life, and contained them within its specific category.

The more I denied and hid these negative parts of myself, the greater was my need to hide behind psychological masks. I found that there was a direct connection between my False Self and my Shadow, since the more internal emptiness was created through denying my negative aspects, the higher the facade of my False Self. In turn, the higher the facade of my False Self, the greater the "shadow" it threw on my inner life.

As my Shadow grew, it engulfed me and made me lose contact with my original core. Often I felt that I was living a lie, because of the huge gap between how other people perceived me and the way I felt inside. I also discovered a paradox of my Shadow. Although I thought I was always positive, the repressed nature of my Shadow had powerful negative effects, not only in my life but also in other people's lives. Not being aware of my "lost" negatives conditioned me to think and do all kinds of things that I could never understand.

A way that we can all recognize the effects of our Shadows in our lives is by becoming aware of the effects that our actions have on other people and in the world in general. While we may at first be unaware of what repressed negativity we have inside of ourselves, we can more easily become aware of negative patterns that are operating in our lives and in other people's lives. For example, in my life my Shadow led to frequent arguments, fights, and constantly hurting other people's feelings. I discovered that I was living as if in the calm "eye" of a hurricane, created by the false positives of my False Self, unaware that I was damaging the lives of the people around me.

I began to practice a technique which helped me to deal with the effects of repressed negativity by creating a time line of major negative events in my life. First I drew a line across a piece of paper. At one end of the line I wrote down the year of my birth. I then summarized, chronologically, the major negative events that occurred during my childhood. Then beginning with the year that I graduated from high school, I wrote down each major negative event that had occurred in my relationships and directly above it the date when it occurred. I ended the time line with the current date. Patterns emerged of how my explosive, sometimes violent temper, had imbued relationships in my life with tension, anxiety and fear. What became apparent to me was that I was living on a roller coaster. When I realized that the "downs" of my life were created by the negative effects of my Shadow, I wrote down what I thought was the cause of each negative pattern on my negative time line, and next to each entry I wrote how my denied negative aspects had affected my relationships with other people.

After doing this exercise I realized that if I didn't change, my hidden but powerful negativity would ensure that the same patterns would repeat themselves for the rest of my life. I also realized that if I did not make fundamental changes in my life, I was going to die at an early age because of all my addictions, stress, and anger which were caused by my hidden negativity. I asked myself, "Is this the way I want to spend the rest of my life?" My answer was a resounding "No!"

Rather than assuming that other people were the cause of my problems, I began to consider the possibility that I was at the root of them. Also, rather than assuming that negativity is "bad" and to be avoided at all cost, I came to understand that my negativity actually provided me with a context, a "cutting edge," for my personal growth. It was extremely helpful to discover that one's negativity can be an inherent part of the evolutionary process of personal transformation.

"Shadow Talk"

I discovered that my repressed negativity expressed itself in my life as an inner voice whose "language" consisted of critical, negative and limiting messages. This all too familiar, critical voice was constantly being played, at a low frequency, in my unconscious. B.T., whenever I decided to make positive changes in my life, tried to do something unfamiliar or felt vulnerable and exposed, the negative messages of my "Shadow Talk" increased to such a high frequency that I could literally hear them. These messages led to a lack of conviction and feelings of uncertainty that created a general doubt about my abilities, minimizing the value I had of myself and making me question what I had to offer the world.

My Shadow also contributed to my fear of success. When I began achieving success, I would hear messages that I did not deserve success. When I pulled back so that my degree of success was brought back to a level that was comfortable to my Shadow, I would then experience a sense of comfort, which often led to a renewed sense of purpose and enthusiasm which I used to begin the self–defeating process all over again. It wasn't until I acknowledged my Shadow that I was able to accept myself as truly worthy of success.

Not acknowledging my "Shadow" also had a negative effect on my personal relationships. Often when a relationship was going well, especially with a woman, I would say or do something that caused a fight. During my inner journey I discovered that my denied negativity caused anxiety within me, because I knew that the positive, confident, secure "me" that the other person saw was not the person that I experienced deep inside. The less intimacy I allowed, the less the chance that the other person could see beyond my False Self.

My negativity also caused me to feel tension when a relationship was going smoothly. A persistent question I asked myself, which originated in my Shadow was: "If I don't love myself, what's wrong with this other person who loves me?" Getting into an argument made the level of the relationship drop back down into my Shadow's "comfort zone." The fight also confirmed that my inner negative perception, and not the high positive perception of the other person, was correct. As with my "fear of success," I often felt a renewed sense of purpose in the relationship during the making up process. Normally the relationship would go into an upward swing until the next time that the tension between the positive relationship and my denied negativity became unbearable again.

Appendix 1 shows how to create a "Shadow Talk Journal" which can help you to recognize and change the self–destructive patterns and negative influences of your Shadow.

Exploring my Shadow brought me numerous benefits. Most important, it helped me regain my balance and innate wholeness. I also found that the more I incorporated the negative aspects of who I was into my being, the more confident and complete I felt.

Doing my Shadow work allowed me to confront, rather than evade, what I most feared. Accepting the unacceptable and owning the destructive aspects of myself, which I had denied for so long, allowed me to greatly reduce the feelings of shame, guilt and insecurity that were generated from within my Shadow. Exploring my Shadow also led to increasing my energy, since it was no longer being wasted in denial and repression. After awhile I experienced joy during my healing process by becoming aware of my "disowned self;" I was discovering an inherent but long lost part of who I was.

An analogy of a person not being aware of the negative aspect of his life is a seesaw which is weighed down on one side–the negative. Lessening the "weight" of my negativity by expanding my awareness to recognize and accept my Shadow allowed my life to regain its natural balance. I also found that the more I became aware and accepting of the contents of my Shadow, the more spiritual I felt, since I was becoming re–connected with my soul. The sense of empowerment created by the process of discovering my authentic self allowed me to become more tolerant first toward myself and then toward other people.

Exploring the Shadow

Since each of us has had different life experiences, the contents of your Shadow will in many ways be different from mine. Yet most of us share some similarities, in part because of our common cultural conditioning. Also, the experience of being separated from our original center leads to a host of familiar personality characteristics—often called "defenses"—which are common to most of us in varying degrees.

Before I acknowledged my Shadow, I projected my negatives outward by criticizing and blaming others. This bolstered my False Self with its illusions of perfection and power. When I began to acknowledge and explore my Shadow, I was astonished to discover fear, guilt, shame, vulnerability, neediness, and lack of self–esteem—exactly the opposites of the False Self I had created.

These negative feelings were so painful that for most of my life, B.T., I had to cover them up and compensate for them through the overblown illusions of my False Self. Only by accepting them was I released from their grip, which enabled me to create new, positive alternatives leading to a sense of healthy self–love.

Since feelings of fear, shame, and vulnerability are common to so many of us who are disconnected from our original healthy inner core, I will describe in more detail how these feelings expressed themselves in my life, and how I was able to loosen their unacknowledged power over me.

Fear

Fear, with its associated feelings of anxiety and insecurity, was actually an all–pervading emotion within my Shadow. Fear caused me to lose my innate balance and colored my relationship both with myself and the rest of the world. You might ask, Isn't fear good in a life-threatening situation? The answer is no. We were all born with an innate fight–or–flight reaction when threatened, but fear actually increases the threat of serious injury or death by causing us to freeze or panic in times of danger.

Fear, which often paralyzed my life, B.T., expressed itself in various forms. When I was a young child, a general atmosphere of anxiety dominated my environment. From the people around me I learned to have restless, uneasy feelings toward the world in general, often over some indefinite but anticipated "bad things" that could happen to us in the future. *Tabor's Medical Dictionary* lists 211 fears, ranging from fear of air (aerophobia), to the fear of strangers (xenophobia). The father of them all is the fear of death (thanatophobia), which is associated with the fear of punishment, darkness, and the unknown. Fear strengthens all our other negative images and belief systems, and perpetuates the fear of change. It keeps us from reaching out, taking chances, and making changes. Many of us even fear success. Secretly, we may feel we are not worthy of success, or we may fear the envy of others if we succeed.

Fear is also the major cause of procrastination, the tendency to put off doing things. In a wonderful little pamphlet called *The Common Denominator of Success*, Albert E.N. Gray, who observed hundreds of very successful salespeople, discovered that hard work alone did not lead to success. Successful people do the things that people who fail do not want to do, and put off by procrastinating. People who procrastinate will create all kinds of reasons to justify their inaction, such as fear of failure, of doing a poor job, of making a fool of oneself, of being judged unfairly; or perhaps the fear of doing a good job, or fear of success. Both fear of success and fear of failure prevent us from going after what we really want to do in life.

Shame

Shame was also a pervasive emotion in my Shadow. I realized that shame, which Dr. Andrew Morrison, author of *The Culture of Shame,* defines as "a feeling of intrinsic self–worthlessness,"[6] evolved as conditioned images and feelings inside myself, because since childhood I had been told in many ways that I was inherently unworthy.

Shame causes you to feel loathing towards yourself, and leads to feelings of incompetence, isolation, separation, and insecurity. These deep feelings of insecurity and vulnerability were the basis of my existence until I chose to transform my inner self. My various addictions were actually attempts to anesthetize my painful feelings of shame and the fundamental pain of disconnection from my original nature.

The psychological process of internalization explains that we take in the qualities and mindsets of our caretakers—from our parents, grandparents and other relatives and mentors during infancy and childhood. Their judgments, values and criticisms helped form our concept of ourselves. Thus, if our caretakers felt weak and insecure, we as infants picked up and learned these feelings. Furthermore, in my family my parents valued what the neighbors thought, more than they valued what I felt and who I was. If I had learned a healthy, balanced approach, I would have learned to value my own needs as well as meet the needs of others. But because I had no inner basis for strength or healthy self–love, I protected myself by becoming self–involved and preoccupied with meeting my own selfish needs, and at the same time feeling isolated, unloved, and incapable of giving.

I was also taught moral shame, and thus felt inherently defective. For example, if as a child I spilled some milk or a cup accidentally fell, the adult's response was, "What's wrong with you?" or "Why can't you watch what you are doing?" As I internalized my mother's critical voice, I accepted that I was guilty and shameful, and I held such judgments against myself for the rest of my life—until my transformation. This belief in my inherent unworthiness triggered feelings of incompetence, fear of being wrong, and the compulsive need for perfection.

My early beliefs and convictions became the basis upon which I built my adult life. As an infant and child I did not question what adults were teaching me. I automatically incorporated the convictions of my parents and other caretakers, absorbing their feelings of shame and negativity just as they had absorbed these same core beliefs from *their* caretakers. The net result was that I grew up feeling incapable of goodness and love, which in turn reinforced many destructive behavior patterns later in my life.

Emotional Numbing and Low Self–Esteem

As a child I pushed to have my needs met, but this was potentially dangerous. In my childhood, love was given conditionally, usually only when I met the "security needs" of the adults around me. When I became an adult, emotional and sometimes physical separations reinforced my childhood experience of the withdrawal of love. In order to survive as a child, I was wise to understand that I had to repress those feelings and needs which upset my parents.

But the cost of self–repression was high, resulting in alienation from myself, the development of many patterns of denial and repression, and ultimately the limitation of my inner potential. Our childhood relationships with our caretakers also influence our sense of security, trust, and self–esteem. Infants who receive affirming self–acceptance from their adult caregivers develop a firm, positive sense of self, and go on to value, appreciate, and accept both themselves and others. However, by being punished and demeaned, we are conditioned to develop feelings of low self–esteem, which may last for the rest of our lives.

I discovered early in life that it was in my best interests to ignore what I felt inside, since my feelings were unimportant to anyone else. Yet by neglecting my feelings, starting with my inner pain, I lost the ability to express my emotions naturally. Growing up as a man in this culture distanced me even further from my innate feelings. Often the only emotion that I was able to feel and express was rage.

Even today, when someone asks me what I want to do, I am often incapable of answering, since for so long I lived disconnected from my needs and feelings. My usual response is to answer the question with a question, by asking what the other person wants to do. Constantly placing value only on other's needs and feelings also caused me to be deceitful, because I disregarded and denied my own feelings and needs, which further undermined my sense of self–worth. I spent my life B.T. oversensitive to other people's needs, and totally ignoring my own real needs.

Greed

I also recognized that I was driven by greed. My greed for external possessions was motivated by my intense insecurity. I found that it was far easier to expend my energies gathering possessions than to examine my inner life or become aware of how negative images and emotions had created insecurity and a deep inner void. I gained a false sense of security by acquiring material objects, assuming that the more wealth or possessions I owned, the greater my chance for security and happiness. I thought my inner void would be filled, but it didn't work. I was like a person who is constantly stuffing his mouth with food but is never satisfied. Unfortunately, during the past 15 years greed has been institutionalized as a national virtue in this country, and those who express it openly are often held up as role models.*

Creating Positive Alternatives to the Shadow

In addition to becoming aware of and accepting my Shadow, I also had to take responsible action to transform my inner self by creating positive alternatives to my negativity. By creating an attitude of loving awareness and accepting my negatives, yet feeling compassion both for myself and others whom I had hurt, I could spend my time and energy creating positive alternatives, which would balance my negatives and allow me to become centered and whole. I utilized a variety of techniques to accomplish this, starting with visualization.

Visualization

Visualization, which refers to creating images in our minds of what we want to achieve in reality, is a powerful process used by many creative people. For example, when Michelangelo carved his famous sculpture David, he did not impose a design on the marble,

---

*See Appendix A for exercises to help explore your Shadow.

but rather visualized David, then created him out of a defective slab of marble which had been rejected many times over by other sculptors. When Albert Einstein was 16 years old, he visualized himself riding a beam of light, traveling 186,000 miles per second. Years later he put this sensory image into mathematical terms, thus creating the General Law of Relativity.

Many high achievers, including successful athletes, use visualization. I vividly remember watching high jumper David Stone using visualization during the 1984 Los Angeles Olympics. As he stood on the track, Stone visualized himself running, leaping, jumping over the high bar, winning the gold, and creating new world records. He traced every step in his mind, and then did in real life what he had just visualized.

The power of visualization was also demonstrated by Australian psychologist Alan Richardson. He studied three randomly chosen groups of students, none of whom had ever practiced visualization. The first group went out onto a basketball court and physically practiced making free throws every day for 20 days. The second group physically practiced free throws only on the first and twentieth days, but in addition they *visualized* sinking baskets for twenty minutes all the other days. The third group only practiced physically on the first and twentieth days, and did no visualization. The results of the study showed the power of visualization. The first group, which practiced physically every day, improved 24 percent. The second group, which practiced physically only two days, but used visualization the rest of the time, improved 23 percent. The third group showed no improvement at all. [7]

Visualization could be described as "practicing in one's imagination." As Dr. Maxwell Maltz explains in *Psycho–Cybernetics,* by using the power of imagination, "for all practical purposes, you are creating a *practice* experience. And if the imagination is vivid enough and detailed enough, your imagination practice is equivalent to an experience, insofar as your nervous system is concerned."[8] Furthermore, Dr. Maltz wrote, "the price for having a negative self–image inhibits our abilities, frustrates our God–given talents, and allows us to suffer anxiety, fear, self–condemnation and self–hate. We literally choke off the life force available to us and turn our backs upon the gift which our Creator has made. The degree that we deny the gift of life, we embrace death."[9]

What we picture in our mind's eye—what we feel and believe inside—creates our personal reality. When my image of myself was negative, it made it hard to do positive things for myself. I needed to create a balance to my existing negative mental pictures, and their negative emotions, by replacing them with positive mental images and their associated positive feelings. I used the analogy of a pond to begin creating positive alternatives. The water of a pond, which symbolized my life, was constantly being disturbed by the rippling effect of negative rocks thrown into it. I imagined throwing positive rocks into the same pond. Their rippling effect acted as an interference pattern which balanced the negative rippling effect. (See Figure 3.1.)

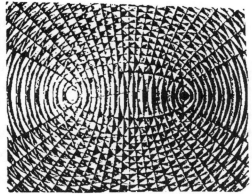

Figure 3.1.

Visualization allowed me to actively transform myself by "reprogramming" my internal imagery. When I became aware of a negative characteristic or behavior in my Shadow, I would visualize what I would feel like instead, and how I would act if its complementary positive were in my life. I practiced visualizing vivid positive images of myself. Creating clear mental images with very specific details greatly strengthened my visualization process. The key was to create extremely detailed pictures, since the more I "felt" and "saw" the new positive image, the more the new mental imagery was strengthened and the greater the results in actual life. I also reinforced these mental images by cutting out magazine pictures which showed in detail what I wanted to accomplish, and pasting them up where I could see them every day. For five minutes each day I used the power of my imagination to create detailed mental images of myself feeling, acting, and being in a positive way. As these new, positive mental images became more real to me, I would then ask myself what practical things did I need to do in order to create this new person in reality?

I had never known what my own needs were, since I had always been trained to meet the needs of others at my own expense. To break out of this scenario I first needed to create vivid pictures on my mental screen of what my own real needs were. Besides finding out what my neglected needs were, I needed to take responsible action for fulfilling them, since our actions support and maintain the images and opinions that we have of ourselves. As a child, I was taught to feel inadequate by hearing that "You are not worth it," "You're no good" or "You'll never amount to anything." As a result, I pulled back and stopped trying to get what I really wanted. To create a counterbalancing image, I pictured myself, in great detail, being worthy to achieve what I really wanted in life, and visualized myself effectively achieving what I really wanted to do.

My feeling that I had no value or worth was reflected in negative images of my body. I had been conditioned into believing that my body was inherently dirty, a vehicle for sin and evil. In the past, especially around the New Year, I might decide to take better care of my body by exercising and eating well, yet after a short time I would stop, because the goal of taking care of myself did not fit with my internal negative self–image. Without a positive body image, I failed to take care of myself though I knew I needed to. To create a positive body image, I needed to decide what I realistically wanted to look like, and then ask myself what practical things I needed to do to bring this new body into reality.

I reinforced the creation of a new body image by putting a picture of a body which came closest to what I wanted to look like on the refrigerator. Taking care of myself involved knowing what I wanted to accomplish, picturing what I wanted to look like, believing that I deserved it and that I could do it, then continuously visualizing and doing the required exercises in actuality. Since one of my goals was to lose weight, I congratulated myself as I lost even one to two pounds, which further energized my positive image, since success breeds success.

New Ways of Speaking

I also discovered that how I spoke and what I said were crucial to the creation of a positive self–image and positive beliefs. Patterns of speech either strengthen or diminish our self–images, because what we say is what we hear, which sends either positive or negative messages to our brains. It took time for me to change my ingrained speech patterns, since I first had to become aware of what I was saying. As my positive self–image and beliefs became stronger, my speech patterns became more confident, which further strengthened positive images and beliefs about myself.

For the first time I began to tell people what I was really feeling. In the past, because of my feelings of inferiority, I would often withdraw, remain silent or even agree when I actually disagreed with others' opinions. Realizing that I and my opinions counted helped me to disagree politely when someone did not agree with me. I began to use the word "I" more frequently and with emphasis. When someone gave me credit I would agree with them, rather than saying "Oh, it's nothing." As I spoke with increasing confidence and conviction, it reinforced my being able to value myself and to feel that I was actually worthy of being heard.

Changing Beliefs

Psychologically, our personal universe flows in the general direction of our deep–seated beliefs whether or not we realize we have them. Our personal philosophy is our guide to how we approach everything from routine chores and workday challenges to our deepest goals. I found it helpful to make a list of my assumptions, beliefs, and convictions about myself and the world, since they determined how I lived each day.

Our beliefs affect our ability to act successfully. I discovered that if in my heart I did not really believe or want something, then I acted without conviction and therefore never succeeded. As I became aware of my programmed belief system, I evaluated and eliminated those beliefs which limited the realization of my fullest potential.

When I become motivated I do not give up easily, which was a key strength I needed for transforming my life. When I am positively motivated I am open and willing to make necessary changes, and I do not quit even in the face of old habits and dysfunctional behaviors. The more I established positive images and beliefs about myself, the more I became motivated, which further helped focus my abilities and energies on achieving meaningful personal change. Discipline and self–control helped bring these positive images and beliefs into reality. I also read numerous books on the nature of the Shadow and spirituality, and listened to numerous audio–cassette tapes while driving, since they reinforced a positive way of life.

Positive beliefs and mental images were mutually reinforcing. Creating affirming beliefs allowed me to develop confidence in the successful outcomes of my actions. I developed feelings of certainty, which reinforced the belief that I could accomplish anything I wanted to, since I no longer doubted my abilities. As my new balanced mindset became ever stronger, the stronger my belief grew that I would do whatever was necessary to transform my life even more. The more positive beliefs I developed, the more energy I freed up to make further changes. Four basic beliefs helped me create positive change: "I *can* do it;" "I *want* to do it;" "I *choose* to do it;" and "I *will* do it." I applied this process by asking myself four questions: What can I do? What do I want to do? What do I choose to do? What will I do? And I did whatever was necessary.

Each step in the creation of positive images and beliefs about myself strengthened my heartfelt desire to change my life. A spirit of fearlessness emerged, so that instead of withdrawing, I gained the courage to face and deal with what was difficult and painful in my life. I developed a courage of my convictions, which created a purposefulness of mind, helping me to continue on my inner journey toward finding and expressing my life's real purpose and living from my authentic inner self.*

---

*See Appendix A for exercises to create positive alternatives in your life.

Finding the Authentic Inner Self

Highly motivated people are inherently positive and enthusiastic. They have tapped into an inner meaning by knowing that what they are doing on a daily basis is moving them closer and closer to achieving their personal vision for who they are and what their life is about. A deep sense of meaning developed in my life by knowing that I was becoming attuned to my true inner purpose. Writing a personal mission statement allowed me to identify and move onto my life's true path. Mission statements are used in any well–run business as a constant reminder of the purpose of the organization, to keep it on track. In the same way, my personal mission statement gave my life clear direction. Realizing that mission statements can be hard to write, since often the simplest things can also be the hardest, I asked myself two questions: "What do I want to accomplish in the remaining days of my life?" and "What am I going to do to make this happen?" The answers to these questions helped me write out my personal mission statement.

As the process of transformation became more real and far–reaching, I began to regain a sense of the true nature of my authentic inner self. This authentic self has the following characteristics:

1. I no longer feel defective, since I value love, feel worthy of love and capable of loving others.
2. I am more tolerant, accepting, and compassionate toward other people.
3. I am connected to the humor and playfulness of life.
4. I feel more connected to the larger universe, and now experience and feel connected to a cosmic source of love.
5. I feel authentic passion, meaning, and purpose in my life. I

realize that my innermost goal is to share with other people
my new understanding about the universe and our purpose
here, which is to claim and express our own unique gifts,
and share love and compassion with others.

I believe that this authentic self has always been with me—in
fact, I was born with this self—but it became disconnected from me
and buried under the negative experiences and negative programing
I subsequently encountered as I grew up. As I continued to balance
my Shadow with new positives, the defensive walls and limitations
of my False Self fell away, and my original self gradually
re–emerged.

I developed a symbolic image which helped me visualize and
continue on this transformation process. (See Figure 3.2.)

How the False Self and Shadow Bury the Authentic Inner Self

My False Self:

E

⊕ My False positives (projected outward)

My limited awareness

⊖ My unrecognized negatives
(projected onto others)

O

Authentic Self:
Disconnected from and hidden
beneath my False Self

Figure 3.2.

Note that this image is vertical—hierarchical—with the imbalanced

Note that this image is vertical—hierarchical—with the imbalanced False Self on top, and the Authentic Self disconnected and located at the bottom. As my self–transformation process continued, this symbolic representation also changed—in its orientation (from vertical to horizontal), in its components and scope, and in their relationship to each other. The chapters to come will describe this process, this changing image, and the meaning of each successive change.

From the False Self to a Healthy Self–Love

A negative sense of self can be created not only through personal experiences of transference of fear and shame, but also through a basic cultural misunderstanding.

Many of us think of "self–love" as negative. People who love themselves are assumed to be "conceited" or even "sinful." But in fact there is an enormous difference between selfishness and self–love. Selfishness—the tendency to be self–centered, to view everything in relation to oneself, to consider only oneself and one's own interest, and to use others only for one's self–advancement—is a defense which arises from a negative self–image and disconnection from one's true power and inner core.

Unfortunately, in our culture, if a child (or even an adult) experiences a wonderful feeling of self–importance, which includes joy in oneself and pleasure at being uniquely oneself and being alive, he is considered proud, vain, or conceited. Children are often denied deserved praise due to the mistaken belief that they will develop a "fat head." An emerging island of self–love is swallowed up by a sea of negativity.

As I reconnected with my true inner self, I learned that we can experience ennobling sensations of loving ourselves, resulting from such actions as honest achievement, genuine self–discipline, and open–hearted sharing. I cannot repeat often enough the vital necessity of creating centered individuals, unafraid of self–love, because people who truly love themselves have no need to tear other people down, and are able to feel and express genuine love for others.

Personal Transformation as a Paradigm Shift

Each of us is a unique individual, yet each of us is also influenced both by other individuals and the larger culture around us. The intense personal work I did to discover my Shadow and create positive alternatives to it took place inside myself, yet many of the belief systems that I discovered in my Shadow came from others, both in my family and as cultural messages through teachers, the media, etc. Furthermore, as I transformed myself as an individual, this affected not only how I felt about myself, but also how I acted and related to the people around me. So even though my transformation started at the individual level, it is interconnected with and affects a much larger world than mine alone.

My definition of success had a great deal of influence on my attitudes, behaviors, and what I valued in life B.T. I was brought up to believe that success meant only the externals of status, position, power, and possessions. In fact, competition was my way of life. I loved the challenge, strategizing, and doing whatever had to be done in order to win. Competition focused and energized me around the only thing that mattered in my life—winning. I felt competitive with almost every other man I met, playing a constant game of one–upmanship.

Through my journey into inner awareness, I discovered that my driving need for high achievement was a psychological consequence of having been disconnected from my original emotions and needs. The need to achieve external success helped me feel important and of value, and I experienced a temporary sense of positive self–esteem whenever I successfully achieved my goals. This sense of achievement never lasted long however, because it was not connected to anything positive inside of me.

I was conditioned to always keep busy, focusing on the external, superficial details of the day. I always had to have something to do. Overemphasizing the external never allowed me to slow down or take the time to focus my awareness inwardly. Looking inward felt scary, was a waste of time, something to be avoided at all costs. I used to dread Sundays especially, when the stores were closed, because there was nothing for me to do. Why would I want to slow down? If I connected with myself, I might become aware of something unpleasant that had been locked away for years. It was much safer to stay numbed out by television, shopping, golf, whatever, as long as it consumed my time and kept me too busy to know myself.

Like most men in our society I was conditioned to believe that a man's value is measured by how big his bank account is or how expensive his clothes, house, cars, boats, etc. are. Also, having the best looking woman at your side, "a trophy woman," was an indicator of success. B.T., my language both in business and in my personal life was markedly aggressive. "I'm going to take his head off," "Attack, attack, always attack," or "Pick and choose your battles," were phrases I often used.

get angry at anything and anyone I felt was preventing me from obtaining what I wanted. The people around me never knew when what they did might trigger my violent temper, and they constantly felt as if they were "walking on eggshells." When I got angry, most people would back down, giving me whatever it was I wanted.

Paradoxically, I also became a "pleaser." As a child I learned that my very survival was dependent upon meeting the needs of my adult caregivers (instead of the other way around). When I was young, if I tried to assert myself, to express myself or ask for what I needed, I was punished psychologically or physically. Over time I lost touch with my own needs, learning instead that only the other person's needs were important.

As an adult I became extremely proficient at determining others' emotional needs, which enabled me to manipulate them to meet *my* needs. For example, I became an expert at stroking the ego needs of physicians, which led to my success in medical sales. Also I became a Casanova so I could use women for sexual pleasure. I often used my "pleasing" persona when I wanted to get something from another person, while I used anger to control people.

B.T., I did not have personal relationships in the true sense of the word. The essence of relationships is connection, and B.T. I did not feel a sense of connection either with myself or with other people. I had learned to value being a "man's man," which meant being focused on external matters. Men who expressed their feelings were considered "soft," not respected as "real men," and the world of feelings and relationships was considered "women's stuff," of no worthwhile value. Because I was so bad at relationships, I used achievement to compensate, because it was one area in my life that I could control. Whenever a personal relationship was going bad, I could control. Whenever a personal relationship was going bad, I would spend more time working. The more a personal relationship deteriorated, the more successful I became professionally.

Relationships deal with feelings, and the last thing I wanted to do was become aware of my feelings. The dysfunctional relationships that I had experienced and observed during my life B.T. were often a source of pain, so why should I value them? The most effective strategy was avoidance. Not being interested in relationships allowed me to avoid addressing the issues inside me which contributed to my problems in the first place. In my relationships with other people B.T., I can see now that I was anxious, afraid of diversity, argumentative, a user and a taker, blaming, conceited, cynical, fearful, greedy, humorless, insecure, intolerant, isolated, judgmental, narrow–minded, opinionated, always serious, selfish, and disconnected from what I was feeling. As I continued to do personal work, my inner awareness gradually became transformed. This enabled me to recognize and accept the negative aspects of my personality, which I had previously denied and repressed.

I now realize that everyone and everything on this planet is in the process of changing and growing. Developing an evolutionary process orientation eliminated my need for perfection, which had been driven by my unrecognized low self–esteem. I now know that my life is, and always will be, a work in progress.

I am still dealing with the psychological effects of the weight of negativity in my life. Even though I have done an enormous amount of transformational work, I still have hurts and pains which were created over the years by negativity. I still get upset when I feel that I am being criticized. What is different is that rather than automatically reacting to hurt, I am now aware that I am in the process of getting upset, which is a huge achievement in itself. By accepting that my "old buttons" are being pushed, I am able to take responsibility for where I am emotionally, and I either explain to the other person that I am getting upset, or I walk away, creating the space which allows my negative feelings to dissipate.

An analogy I have found useful in the process of eliminating the burden of negativity is an evergreen shrub which is bent over to one side by the weight of wet, heavy, accumulated snow. In my case I was bent over toward the negative through the weight of much negative conditioning and the resulting accumulation of negative experiences in my life. Gradually, as the sun melts the snow, the shrub periodically jerks upwards, eventually regaining its rightful, straight position. As the light of awareness removed the heavy weight of the negative contents of my Shadow, I too gradually moved to my natural upright position.

This resulted in creating meaningful changes in my life. First, I worked on the obstacles which I had ignored for many years which had been blocking my personal growth. I became aware that so many of my past actions were motivated by fear and insecurity. I gained the ability to break out of fear and insecurity, and began to center my life on love rather than fear. I connected with the two basic aspects of my personality—the male and female—both of which exist within each of us. I generally stopped categorizing and stereotyping people. I moved beyond a dualistic, either/or mentality to a more wholistic understanding of reality. I balanced my competitive spirit with a spirit of cooperation. My compassion for other people, and for all living things, increased markedly. I worked hard to allow the quality of kindness to emerge in my personality. I now consciously strive to be sympathetic, friendly, gentle, tender–hearted, generous, pleasant, considerate, and thoughtful, and am proud to have people think of me in this way. I started allowing myself to make mistakes instead of blaming other people, became less dogmatic about my opinions, and instead grew more tolerant of other points of view. I stopped pretending that I had all the answers. Surprisingly, as all these changes happened I found that I no longer needed to justify my life to others. The less I needed to control other people and events, the more I began to take control of my own thoughts and actions.

As I integrated my head with my heart and my intelligence with my good intentions in my relationship with myself and interactions with other people, I went from being a monologuer to being a dialoguer. The quality of my relationships improved even more as I gained the ability to listen, the key to effective communication, since I no longer needed to always be thinking of what I was going to say while the other person was speaking. Because my mind is no longer closed by defensiveness, I am now able to listen to what the other person is really saying. I am also more able to listen intently to what other people have to say because I now have more respect for other people, and I am more able to interact authentically with each new person, as a unique individual. I have also stopped using "should's," "could's," and "would's"—the vocabulary of judgment and control—in my conversations with other people.

In addition, my energy and efficiency increased markedly. I am now genuinely enthusiastic about whatever I am doing. Enthusiasm is a strong emotion which has a compelling effect in one's life, since other people intuitively pick it up. I am pleased to generate an excitement in my eagerness to share my passion for life and growth with others.

B.T., I rarely ever laughed, and the little humor I expressed had an edge to it because I took my life so seriously. A.T. , I laugh much more because now I find humor in so many things that I never did before. I now believe that humor is a characteristic of divinity, since that paradox is a fundamental characteristic of the universe. I enjoy being so much funnier and wittier.

I now experience the wonder of life and the joy of living. Watching the natural joy of children or animals playing helped reawaken my own sense of joy. I experience joy simply in having another day of life, having the opportunity to participate in the creative play of life. I feel joy for just being able to see the sun rise each morning and know that I am privileged, because one day the sun will rise and I will no longer be here to see it or to experience what it means to be alive on this planet.

Finally, I achieved my personal goal of 20 years, which was to understand the next evolutionary level of consciousness. B.T, I always needed to know exactly what was going to happen, since I never wanted to be surprised. Deciding that I could let go of my need for control, freed up a tremendous amount of time and energy. One of the many rewards of giving up control was gaining a sense that my life was being guided at a higher level. This has brought about a mystical quality to my life, and I now feel connected with something much larger than myself. Whenever I turn my attention inward and ask for guidance, I feel that I receive it.

Developing a cosmological perspective has eliminated the feeling that my life was unimportant and insignificant. A living cosmology has filled me with a sense of meaning and purpose as I realize that nothing I do is trivial, since my life is part of a fifteen to twenty billion year history of the universe, connected with the ultimate mystery of creation.

Chapter 4

The Balanced Paradigm:
Cosmic Principles for Self–Transformation

Beyond the Mechanistic Paradigm:
The "New Science"

During the time I was going through my personal transformation process, I became ever more fascinated by the latest developments in scientific thought and research, especially with regard to the nature of the universe—from the largest speculations about the origin of the cosmos to the findings about the smallest building blocks which construct our everyday world. I had never been interested in science before then, but as part of my personal transformation, this new interest in science emerged. I learned that over the last 400 years our modern worldview developed, strongly influenced by what is now called the "modern scientific paradigm." Two major seventeenth century thinkers—the mathematician Rene Descartes and the physicist Isaac Newton—helped shape modern science. Both Descartes and Newton were strongly influenced by the emerging mechanical technology of their times, such as the mechanism of the clock, which after being wound up continues to move on its own.

For Descartes, mind and body were completely separate and all living things were simply machines: even the human body was a machine, tenuously connected to a rational soul. Newton expanded this fragmented, mechanistic view of the individual to describe the entire universe. According to Newton, the universe was made up of dead, empty space, in which separate material entities occasionally collided, affected by such forces as gravity and inertia.

Our understanding of space and time shapes our models of reality. Newton wrote that "absolute space, in its own nature, without regard to anything external, always remains similar and immovable." In this model, space is an unchanging, cold, dark void. Bertrand Russell expressed the psychological implications of this worldview in excruciatingly painful language; in relation to the universe he felt a "terrible loneliness in which one shivering consciousness looks over the rim of the world into the cold, unfathomable abyss."[10]

Our model of reality is also based on our concept of time. Newton believed that time, which is separate from space, is "absolute, true and mathematical time of itself and by its own nature, which flows uniformly, without regard to anything external." Newton's concept of the separation of space and time contributed to the fundamental assumption in the modern Mechanistic Paradigm that our lives and everything else in the universe are inherently separate, unconnected.

During the twentieth century, science has once again been undergoing a vast revolution, and leading scientists are now proposing that our health is affected by our minds as well as our bodies; the universe is an intelligent, even spiritual phenomenon; the universe and everything in it are constantly changing and evolving; and everything in the universe is interconnected. As the physicist Paul Davies recently wrote in *The Cosmic Blueprint*:

> There is a widespread feeling among physicists that their subject is poised for a major revolution. As already remarked, true revolutions in science are not rapid advances in technical details, but

transformations of the concepts upon which science is based. In physics, revolutions of this magnitude have occurred twice before. The first was the systematic development of mechanics by Galileo and Newton. The second occurred with the theory of relativity and the quantum theory at the beginning of this century. [11]

The third revolution in science is now underway, as revolutionary transformations are taking place in every area of science today. For this reason, I talk about the discoveries of the "New Science." As I continued to read about the latest developments in physics, biology, medicine, astronomy and cosmology, and new approaches in quantum physics, systems thinking, and chaos theory, I realized that these new scientific principles, processes, and revelations not only resembled the new insights I was acquiring, but actually described the processes and phenomena which I had personally experienced through self–transformation.

The Transforming Universe

We now understand that the history of the universe itself is the history of constant transformation. This process started 15 billion years ago, at the end of the "Fireball," when the universe performed its first transformation by changing from an undifferentiated "soup" of baryons and simple nuclei to the primordial atoms of the elements hydrogen and helium. Some five billion years ago the supernova explosion of the star Tiamat gave birth to the rest of the elements, from which were formed our Earth, all the other planets in our solar system, and the atoms which make up our bodies. Like the larger universe, Earth has always been and still is in the process of transforming itself.

The latest discoveries of modern physics and the New Science talk about such concepts as change, uncertainty, randomness, even chaos as essential principles of reality. This is in direct contrast to the Newtonian, mechanistic model of reality, which assumed and valued certainty and predictability. For example, the influential eighteenth–century mathematician Pierre Simon de Laplace, asserted that human beings were completely predetermined under the mechanical laws of nature, which means that everything that happens in our lives has one single cause, which gives rise to one specific result. In recent years Laplace's determinism has been replaced by the scientific understanding of the nature of randomness which, among other things, allows for human free will even in a universe governed by law. James Gleick, author of *Chaos,* writes that "relativity eliminated the Newtonian illusion of Absolute Space and Time; quantum theory eliminated the Newtonian dream of a controllable measurement process; and chaos eliminates Laplace's fantasy of deterministic predictability." [12]

Scientists have now discovered that uncertainty is an intrinsic characteristic of the most fundamental aspects of the universe, and that change and fluctuation are the ingredients from which order is created. Where Newtonian science found only chaos, the New Science has discovered patterns and commonality. This new approach is known as "dynamical systems theory," "network dynamics," "nonlinear dynamics," or the "theory of complexity."

Scientists now recognize that chaos, or randomness, is essential for the very existence of life. You exist because of the mating of a single sperm from your father with a single egg from your mother, based solely on random chance. Evolution requires genetic variability, which is brought about by chaos, a means of structuring random changes. As Richard Grossinger writes in *Embryogenesis:*

If a perfect transcription of genetic material simply recurred, life would remain static. There would be no parade of living creatures, only identical crystalline forms....The fact that the code is written in amino acid, rather than precise blueprints for organisms, protects life. Because the code has not contained final stage information, it can be *random* without being totally degraded.[13]

Not only your individual creation, but also the continuance of your life depends upon chaotic irregularity and unpredictability. Until recently, medical science believed that physiological systems operated on the principle of "homoeostasis," the theory that any system operates so as to reduce variability. According to that theory, if a system is perturbed by external forces it will become "abnormal," but will return to a "normal" steady state as quickly as possible. Recent discoveries in medicine and physiology have determined that totally regular behavior is actually a characteristic of aging and disease, while variability is associated with good health. For example, it now appears that the mechanism which controls the rate of our heartbeat may be intrinsically chaotic, that under normal circumstances the heart rate may fluctuate considerably, rather than maintaining a homeostatic, steady state.[14]

Change is an inherent ingredient from which order is created. Chaos is also described as "emergent order." The New Science has discovered that chaos is order without predictability—that is, chaos has a hidden order and hidden patterns of complexity.

The New Science has also discovered that when a system in equilibrium goes into chaos, a new, higher order of organization eventually emerges, since coherent behavior naturally emerges at critical points of instability in states of non–equilibrium. A detailed description of self–organizing systems was provided by Nobel Laureate for Chemistry Ilya Prigogine, who was fascinated by the observation that living organisms are able to maintain their life processes under conditions of non–equilibrium. After years of research, Prigogine developed his theory of system self–organization, based on the fact that even systems which are far from equilibrium are still ordered. Prigogine asserts that there is "order through fluctuation."

Self–organizing living systems are *open systems*. Newtonian physics recognized only closed systems, which follow the second law of thermodynamics: that is, entropy (increasing disorder) will build up in a system over time, eventually causing "heat death" to that system. In such closed systems, heat and friction are associated with waste and system breakdown. However, the New Science explains that life is an open, "dissipative system," that is, a structure in which dissipation leads to order and an open, dissipative system may actually evolve to a higher level of complexity.

We now understand that life is an example of a "self–organizing system." Living systems are inherently creative, adaptive, and meaning–seeking, and are able to change themselves in order to continue living. According to the Chilean neuroscientist Humberto Maturana, "Living systems...[are] organized in a closed causal circular process that allows for evolutionary change in the way the circularity is maintained, but not for the loss of the circularity itself."[15] The circular organizational principle of living systems is also a network pattern. Circular systems create life because the function of each component helps produce and transform other components, while maintaining the overall circularity of the network. Francisco Varela collaborated with Maturana to develop a verbal and mathematical model of living systems, based on a process which they called *autopoiesis,* or "self-making." The autopoietic organization of living systems creates a boundary which confines the operations of the network and defines the system as a whole unit.

Scientists have now identified four inherent characteristics of self–organizing systems: such systems are self–creating, self–defining, self–referencing, and self–regulating. Freedom and adaptability are essential for self–organizing systems. They are so loosely constructed that they are at the edge of being out of control, but they continue to maintain dynamic form. They also have the capacity for continuous change. Self–organizing systems actually create new structures and processes which enable them to meet their needs as they arise, or as their environment changes.[16]

The New Science has shifted our understanding of the universe and its components from a focus on structure to an emphasis on flow and process. We now understand that rather than the image of a machine, the metaphor of a flowing river is much closer to the natural process of creation. According to James Gleick, the new science is a "science of process, rather than stasis, of becoming, rather than being."[17] In the old scientific paradigm it was believed that there are fundamental structures which interact through forces and mechanisms which give rise to process. The New Science has discovered that every structure is seen as the manifestation of an underlying process, whose web of relationships is intrinsically dynamic.

The New Science brings us the image of a dynamic, constantly changing and evolving universe, in which living systems are self–organizing, creating new, higher levels of order out of chaos which supports our personal efforts for self–transformation. Its process perspective reassures us that we can let go of long–held beliefs and trust the chaotic discomfort which results, since we know that chaos and seeming formlessness are the fertile ground from which a new, higher order of evolution can emerge. These new findings allow us to have a positive attitude toward change, which can help us to be more adaptable and flexible in an inherently unpredictable and constantly changing environment.

Eastern philosophy has historically focused on process, in contrast to the structural perspective of the Western intellectual tradition. But the latest discoveries of Western science are increasingly similar to Eastern philosophy. I find it both personally meaningful and spiritually significant that we are living through a time in history when the Western scientific tradition—the left brain—is being unified with the Eastern mystical tradition—the right brain. I believe that the outcome of this unification will be the creation of a new, global consciousness for humanity.

The New Science and a New Spirituality

The New Science implies a very different concept of God, and a very different approach to spirituality than the belief system in which I was raised. Like many of us, regardless of our specific religions, I was brought up to believe in a dualistic universe, in which the Creator—an all–powerful, judgmental old man with a beard—resides far away, "Up there," and looks down upon us, his imperfect creations. He is the essence of everything good and perfect, while we humans are weak and sinful. In this concept of religion, your happiness and fulfillment depend upon receiving favor from the Almighty which you obtain through prayers, supplication, and even bargaining, ("I'll do this for You, if You do this for me.")

Inner growth is irrelevant in this approach to religion, and inner spirituality does not exist. You are supposed to feel isolated and powerless. The only way to feel good about yourself is to believe in the dogmas, perform the correct external actions, and have faith in the omnipotence of that distant Creator "up there."

This disempowering view of the spiritual nature of the universe, and humanity's place in it, is reinforced by the cosmology implicit in mechanistic Newtonian science. In that view, the universe was compared with a clockwork. In the beginning, God wound it up and set it in motion, then remained separated from it and looked on, giving humans no choice but to obey the mechanistic laws which God had created.

By contrast, the New Science teaches that everything in the universe is connected, and that even we human beings partake of the same atomic matter, patterns of intelligence, and divine creative forces which have created the stars, the planets, and all the rest of the universe. Since in this view, the universe is a dynamic entity, constantly changing and evolving, and we human beings also participate through our personal growth and social evolution in contributing to the evolution of the universe, we are in a sense co-creators of the universe. Since our inner lives and awareness shape our actions, our inner lives are as important as our outer, external lives.

In this new vision, each of us contains within ourselves a powerful creative force. We deepen our spirituality as we recognize our personal connection to the larger universe, and experience and express our innate creativity.

Balance as a Universal Process

Scientists are also discovering that balance—as a dynamic process—is a basic characteristic of the universe. In the Newtonian model, balance is viewed as the result of two opposing forces, which exert equal force on each other. Any extra weight on one side or the other automatically creates an imbalance. Maintaining equilibrium is the desired goal in this static concept of balance, yet it is nearly impossible to maintain balance in this concept, since even a small change on one side will throw the other side off balance. (This static interpretation of balance is also the basis of the foreign policy of nations, where it is called the Balance of Power.) An example of static balance exists in the atmosphere of the planet Mars. Compounds and gases in the Martian atmosphere have settled into a state of equilibrium, which is one reason why no life exists on Mars today. On the other hand, life exists on our planet Earth because the gases in our atmosphere are in a dynamic state of disequilibrium.

In *Design for Evolution* Erich Jantsch writes, "a static world is based on the notions of equilibrium and a dualism between irreconcilable opposites."[18] The New Science has helped expand our concept of balance from a static to a dynamic definition. We now understand that balance is not a static state, but the result of a continuous process of interaction between complementary opposites, which means that *balance implies continuous change*.

The process of dynamic balance has been a basic, recurring theme throughout my personal experience of transformation. Before transformation I was in a static state because my fears caused me to try to control everything around me, keeping the world and my life predictable and "safe." Not only was I trapped in unchanging beliefs and attitudes, I was actually in a state of imbalance, because I was stuck in excessive negativity. Once I committed myself to the personal process of change by looking inward, beyond my "successful" False Self, I discovered my negative, fearful, pain–causing, and self–defeating Shadow. This was my first step toward becoming more balanced, because I was creating a more realistic balance to my falsely positive external self.

As I became more fully aware of my Shadow, I then proceeded

to create positive alternatives to balance its previously hidden negatives. This was my second step toward becoming more balanced, and it helped me gain both greater internal wholeness and greater effectiveness in the external world. But balance is a dynamic process. As I continued the process of awareness, acceptance, and action, I discovered how to reach and stay connected to my personal Center of Balance, which guides me from my deepest core wisdom no matter what twists and turns the world brings. Staying balanced does not mean staying still, but continuing to learn and grow, constantly participating in a "cosmic dance" with my inner self, other people, and the ever changing world around us.

Discovering imbalance and continuing to create balance which does not stop but continues as an underlying process of life and growth, represents a basic process of the universe. The New Science teaches that all aspects of the universe and of life are shaped by *dynamic balance*. For example, a wave is a fundamental and ubiquitous pattern, with its rising crest and descending trough manifesting over and over and over. The wave pattern is reflected everywhere—in the repeated transition from day to night; in numerous biological patterns in our own bodies, such as the heart's constant contraction and expansion and our ongoing experience of breathing in and breathing out; and in every other area of life. (See Figure 4.1.)

Dynamic Balance: The Wave Pattern

Figure 4.1.

Dynamic balance also describes the creative change processes throughout the universe, as its seemingly separate but inherently interconnected parts—from its largest to its most minuscule components—interact, coming together and rebalancing each other in an endless dance. For instance, the weather that we experience daily is created by a dynamic balance between the cyclic pattern of Highs, which bring fair weather, and Lows, which bring stormy weather. There is a dynamic balance between the amount of solar energy absorbed into our atmosphere and the amount of heat which is radiated out. There is a dynamic balance between the amount of rain that falls and the amount of water which evaporates back into the atmosphere, and between the oxygen generated by earth's plants and the carbon dioxide generated by its animals.

Through my spiritual studies, I learned that the concept of balance is also central to many spiritual traditions. For example, in an interview with Bill Moyers on Public Television, Oren Lyons, a faith–keeper of the Six Nation Iroquois Confederacy said, "You are made up of good and evil and you must strike a balance—your spiritual center." Many Eastern traditions use the imagery of a "third eye" which is located in the middle of your forehead, right between your two physical eyes. This "third eye," your eye of wisdom, symbolizes the ability to see the sacredness that exists in our everyday world. By reconnecting with your original Center of Balance, you symbolically open your own sacred third eye and can now "see" the deeper underlying connections which join the various manifestations of creation.

Integrating the New Science
and Personal Transformation

The more I read about the latest developments and discoveries in the "New Science," the more I recognized that my own personal transformation process and my worldview and ways of living A.T. reflected the new principles and processes by which scientists are now coming to understand and describe the universe. This realization affirmed all the hard personal work I had gone through, and validated the new values and worldview I was developing as a result of my transformation. It also gave me a clear new direction for action.

At that point in my life I had two main goals. First, I wanted to continue my personal transformation. The changes I had made so far were astounding and gratifying, but I now wanted a firm basis from which I could continue and reinforce my personal growth process. Second, I wanted to share my discoveries about successful personal growth with other people who were also seeking more meaning and fulfillment in life. Not only was this mission an integral part of my newly–emerged authentic self. Sharing what I had learned, especially through writing a book, would fulfill the promise I had made to Judy when she was dying.

It seemed to me that there must be *universal principles about the nature of reality*—now being discovered by the New Science—which apply both *to the cosmos* in its largest manifestation, and also *to one's personal experience* as an individual human being who is seeking meaningful self–transformation and a more fulfilling way of life.

Up to this point I had been sensing these universal principles intuitively, and applying them to achieve my own transformation.

If I could consciously identify and describe the universal cosmic principles that I had been following, this would not only further help my own growth, it would enable me to share this new paradigm and its process for self–transformation with other people in a more useful, systematic way.

My next goal, therefore, was to recognize and describe these basic principles of the New Science which apply to personal transformation, so that I could develop and share with others a new paradigm for self–transformation and a new model for meaningful living.

The Balanced Paradigm

After extensive research, study, and self–reflection, I identified seven basic principles which integrate the New Science, psychology, and spiritual wisdom, and correlate with the self–transformation process. Together these seven principles make up a philosophy of life, a cosmology, and a model for personal growth that I call the "Balanced Paradigm." Figure 4.2. presents these seven principles, along with a brief explanation of how each principle can be applied to everyday life.

If some of these principles also sound like the ancient wisdom teachings of revered spiritual traditions, that should not be surprising. As I explain in Chapter 8, the most advanced science is now discovering that the principles which describe the nature of reality and the processes of the universe resemble and support the basic teachings and wisdom shared by many spiritual traditions.

The chapters that follow describe in detail each of these seven principles—its scientific and/or spiritual basis, some suggestions or exercises for applying it, and its implications for personal life, spirituality, and social evolution. Although I have placed these seven principles in the order in which they emerged in my life, they are not a linear series of steps. Since everything in the universe is connected, you can start at any one of these principles and work on it, then move to whichever feels like the next one to go to. I urge you to follow your own intuition about where to start and where to end.

From the Balance of Power to the Power of Balance

The Balanced Paradigm has both inner, spiritual, and outer, external applications. It recognizes the power and benefits of modern (Newtonian) science and the technological progress which has brought us to where we are today. The Balanced Paradigm also allows us to balance the prevailing overemphasis on materialism with an awareness of our spiritual nature, so we benefit from the deeper wisdom, values, and guidance of our internal selves.

The concept of balance expressed in the Balanced Paradigm is not static, where two forces go into equilibrium and nothing new happens thereafter. Instead, it is a dynamic process of constantly creating and recreating balance, as you continue to change and grow. The Balanced Paradigm reflects the fact that to be alive as a loving, caring, creative, effective, and spiritual being means that you are constantly growing and changing. As we learn more, integrate new realizations, and continue to grow, our awareness continues to shift and expand, and we constantly establish a new state of balance and wholeness from which to move beyond yet again. No matter what happens to us, no matter what events the world brings to us, we can apply the concept of dynamic balance, seeking to balance ourselves in response to external events. Thus, balance is both an inherent characteristic, and a process which we can use actively in response to the external world. The Power of

The Seven Principles
of the Balanced Paradigm

1. Principle of Mutuality

**The universe is created and maintained through
the dynamic balance of complementary opposites.**

*Application: Transform your thinking from a polarized, either/or
perspective to a balanced way of thinking, since you will find truth on
both sides.*

2. Principle of Association

**At a deeper level, seeming opposites are connected
by a continuum.**

*Application: You don't have to choose between two extremes; you
have many options within the "gray areas."*

3. Principle of Wholeness

**The universe is a coherent whole,
made up of countless integrated, coherent wholes.**

*Application: You become whole as you honor and integrate all parts of
yourself—positive and negative; inner and outer; masculine and
feminine; mind, body, emotions, spirit, etc.*

4. Principle of Centeredness

**Each of us has an original core, or Center of Balance,
which is the key to our authentic self
and inherent spirituality.**

*Application: Through centering, you can reconnect to both your own
inner wisdom and the spiritual power of the universe.*

5. Principle of Dynamic Reversal

**The universe is a constant flow of ever–changing reality,
to which we can respond creatively.**

*Application: You can stay centered no matter what happens, and you
can transform negative experiences into positive outcomes.*

6. Principle of Universal Connectedness

The universe is an intelligent, interconnected reality.

*Application: You can trust the process. As you give up your need to
control, you allow the universe to bring you guidance and miracles.*

7. Principle of Love–in–Action

**We are all interconnected, and our purpose here is to
express love and compassion for all beings
(starting with yourself).**

*Application: Everything you do has an impact. You can actively
express your interconnectedness to all creation through love and
compassion for all, in your personal, work, and community lives.*

Figure 4.2.

Balance is liberating because we understand not only that we will keep on changing, but that in fact we can direct the way we will change.

Paradoxically, at the same time as we experience this constant dynamic process of balance—change—and reestablish a new state of balance, the Power of Balance also refers to the fact that each of us has an eternal unchanging place of peace, calm, and internal balance deep within. We can access this deep inner place—or Center of Balance—at any time, and our ability to do so is one more expression of the Balanced Paradigm. We discover that life is characterized by a constant dynamic flow between the external and the internal; between focusing outward, acting in and having an effect on the external world; then going inward to that deep, calm place for inner direction and connection to the timeless universal consciousness; then moving out again to act in the everyday world.

The Balanced Paradigm transforms the external "Balance of Power" to a new internal "Power of Balance," providing us with a personal source of empowerment which allows each of us to actualize our potential. You do not have to go to some special location or to some higher authority for the Power of Balance to emerge in your life, since it has always been there, within you.

The Power of Balance brings three gifts to assist your transformation. First is the Power of Courage, a power which is inherently yours. The Power of Balance can help you develop a strong belief in yourself as an individual, creating the courage which enables you to stand up to whatever is difficult and push through to completion. It is easy to avoid inner work by uncritically accepting someone else's message and belief system, rather than having the courage to work on your own internal issues. Courage provides you with the freedom to go beyond your fears, so that you can move to places that you have never been before...test your limits...break through barriers. The Power of Balance provides you with the courage to make meaningful, transformational changes in your life.

This courageous attitude brings a second gift: the Power to Change, which allows you to realize that you no longer have to do the "same old, same old," that there are new ways to do "old" things. You begin to see a whole spectrum of alternatives, an expanded range of options. The Power to Change allows you to move beyond what you previously believed to be reality. As you realize that things can be different, the Power of Balance helps you transform your life, since the choices that you make today create your tomorrows.

An expanded awareness of alternatives brings the third gift: the Power to Choose, which means that you have a fundamental right to choose how your life will be. The Power to Choose awakens your power to make your own decisions, rather than letting other people make decisions for you, since you understand that your choices create your life. Even in the most negative circumstances you can still choose your attitude toward those circumstances.

As the Power of Balance emerged from the center of my being, it provided me with the courage to change by allowing me to see that there were alternatives in my life. Balance provided me with the power that was inherently mine as a human being to choose how I wanted to spend the rest of my life. Rather than trying to control everything in my external world in order to create the illusion of security, I have used the Power of Balance to gain true empowerment, by aligning my thoughts and actions with the larger cosmic principles of creation, and opening my life to gifts and opportunities far greater than I could have ever created through my limited, isolated False Self. These same wonderful gifts and opportunities are available to you.

Chapter 5

Moving Beyond Polarization and Disconnection: The Principles of Mutuality and Association

The Limits of Polarized Thinking

Before my transformation, my possibilities were limited by my habitual tendency to engage in polarized thinking, an "either/or" mentality. I saw everything in terms of opposites, one good and the other bad. Of course, everything *I* felt or wanted or did, was always "good" while anyone who disagreed or anything which got in my way was "bad."

This also meant that there were only winners and losers—someone had to be superior and someone had to be inferior. The times that I did not finish in first place I felt lousy, because if I wasn't a winner, then I had to be a loser, which fed into my negative sense of self. I also used to be a sports fanatic, since it reinforced my competitive spirit and reaffirmed my either/or, winner/ loser mentality. Sports fulfilled my need to have an opposing team—an enemy—to hate.

As a logic system, the dualistic way of thinking was created 2,300 years ago by Aristotle. Aristotle's first law of logic is the Law of Contradiction, which states that "A" cannot be both "B" and "Not–B." Aristotle's second law is the Law of the Excluded Middle, which states that "A" must be *either* "B" *or* "Not-B." For example, light is *either* a wave *or* a particle—it cannot be both.

This either/or system of logic leads to an adversarial, polarized, and extremely limited way of thinking and acting which formed the basis of the mentality of my False Self. My false positive projections created the illusion that I was always right, moral, and good. Meanwhile, I projected my denied negatives onto others, which automatically made other people inferior, wrong, evil, hurtful, and responsible for *my* negative behaviors.

Also, during most of my life B.T., I was extremely committed to conventional religion. The either/or aspect of traditional religion contributed to and maintained my dualistic way of thinking. I was brought up to believe unquestioningly that the world was a battleground between the forces of good and evil, between God and the Devil. At the Harvard Divinity School I discovered that this dualistic approach was institutionalized in organized religion starting in Persia in the sixth century B.C. Zoroastrianism, the religion of the Persian Empire, taught that there is an ongoing battle between supreme good and supreme evil. In combination with Aristotelian logic, this tradition helped create the dualistic mindset so characteristic of Western civilization.

My conventional religious experience reinforced this polarizing perspective. I felt a great sense of belonging and solidarity with people of the same faith, and at the same time a sense of superiority over nonbelievers, since I "knew" that *my* faith (whichever faith it happened to be) was the only true way.

Polarized thinking is the mentality of demagogues who seek power and control for themselves. The either/or way of thinking takes the power of choice away from people because everything is viewed from a divisive perspective. A dualistic mentality can only give simplistic, absolute answers to complex issues. This makes it easy for demagogues to mislead people, since there is no middle ground, which makes compromise impossible. Believing that there is only one right and good way automatically makes the other person wrong and evil.

The absolutism of the dualistic mentality spawns crusaders

dedicated to the righteousness of their cause. Dedicated crusaders view each person as either an ally or an enemy, a colleague or an obstacle in implementing whatever they believe to be the absolute truth. Because of the absolutism of their beliefs, dedicated crusaders feel justified in doing anything in order to further their cause.

This either/or perspective also contributes to a war mentality, because it can view only one country as superior, fighting for a righteous cause by having God on its side. The other nation is therefore automatically inferior, evil, Godless, and peopled by sub–humans. Nationalistic war propaganda transforms the worst act a person can possibly do to another human being—killing him—into a virtue.

Dynamic Balance as a Universal Process

The New Science is discovering that the universe is created not out of mutually distinct polarized opposites, but out of mutually complementary opposites, which interact and re–balance each other through the process of dynamic balance. As Menas Kafatos and Robert Nadeau write in *The Conscious Universe*, "in modern physics ...virtually every major advance in physical theories describing the structure and evolution of the universe has been accomplished by the emergence of new complementarities."[19]

The properties of all chemical reactions can only be understood by the complementary aspect of electrons, since atoms of different charges—positive and negative—attract each other, while atoms of the same charge repel each other. *The Conscious Universe* further states that, "Complementarity is the fundamental structuring principle in our conscious constructions of reality."[20]

Quantum physics has discovered that a fundamental "restlessness" exists at the subatomic level of reality. According to quantum physics, matter is always in motion and the entire world of relationships of subatomic particles is intrinsically dynamic. Dynamic is defined by Webster's Dictionary as "energetic...relating to or tending to change."

The latest scientific discoveries in quantum physics from the world of subatomic particles demonstrate that dynamic balance is a fundamental principle of reality. For example, dynamic balance is found in the "heart" of atoms. A strong force is created in nuclear matter when the distance between nucleons, which is what protons and neutrons are called, is about two to three times their diameter; however, when the distance between them is less than that, protons and neutrons will repel each other. Atomic reality exists when there is an optimal balance between the attractiveness of the nucleus and the reluctance of electrons to be confined within atoms.

New discoveries about the nature of space also demonstrate dynamic balance. Newtonian physics considered space in the universe to be empty, filled only with an airy medium called "ether" which allowed the forces of gravity to work. In 1928, Paul A. M. Dirac discovered that the so–called vacuum, or nothingness of space is actually filled with complementary energies that constantly fluctuate. What looks to us like blackness in space is actually made up of active particles which complement each other, since for every positive particle there is a complementary negative particle. If a positive particle has an upward spin, its complementary negative particle has a downward spin. Also, for every positively charged electron in the universe, there is a corresponding, complementary, negatively charged particle called a positron. Electrons move clockwise and create matter, while positrons move counterclockwise and create antimatter.

Another example of dynamic balance and complementarity in

the universe is the modern understanding by physicists of the nature of light. For many years scientists could not decide if light was made up of waves or particles, since sometimes it appeared to have the characteristics of waves and other times the characteristics of particles. Scientists have now concluded that light displays both wave-like and particle-like properties. Dynamic balance is the basis for the life of all the cells in your body, since in each cell there must be a constantly shifting balance between sodium and potassium electrodes. Balance is also needed in your immune system, since in order for you to be in good health there must be a dynamic balance between the formation and the destruction of your red blood cells.

The fundamental importance of dynamic balance is reflected in the cyclic patterns of your body. Every day your body temperature rises and then falls within a range of one or two degrees. You reach your highest temperature level, as well as your highest level of alertness, during the day. The downward cycle occurs at night, when your body temperature and level of awareness decline; they are at their lowest point when you are in a deep sleep. This complementary up–and–down pattern is called your "circadian rhythm."

Moving any part of your body reflects complementarity. When you move one of your fingers, sixty separate muscle impulses are involved in allowing it to move, and an additional sixty separate muscles provide oppositional balance so that your fingers do not move in the opposite direction (until you tell them to). Every part of your body moves by reciprocal inhibition, which means that if you suppress one nerve you automatically stimulate its opposite.

Another example of complementarity is the dynamic process which maintains balance between the number of species within a given area in ever–changing conditions. Take for example the relationship between owls and their prey, mice, within a specific area. If the mouse population substantially increases, owls from other areas will move in and reduce the number of mice. When the original balance between the mouse and owl populations is reestablished, the owls from other territories will return home.

The complementary nature of reality has been described for centuries in Eastern philosophies. For example, the Buddha once gave the "Flower Sermon," which he offered without saying a word. He simply held up a flower to his followers and let the beauty of its complementary patterns speak for themselves.

Philosopher George Doczi explains:

> "If we look closely at a flower, and likewise at other natural and manmade creations, we find a unity and an order common to all of them. This order can be seen in certain proportions which appear again and again, and also in the similarly dynamic way all things grow or are made by a union of complementary opposites....Take for instance a daisy....The florets that make up the pattern, represented by circles, grow at the meeting points of two sets of spirals, which move in opposite directions, one clockwise, the other counterclockwise."[21]

This pattern is depicted in Figure 5.2.

Figure 5.2.

The ancient Chinese philosopher Chung Tzu wrote in the book *Great and Small* that "he who wants to have right without wrong, order without disorder, does not understand the principles of heaven and earth. He does not know how things hang together."

The complementary nature of opposites is reflected in the famous Chinese symbol of Yin and Yang. (See Figure 5.3.) As the *Random House Encyclopedia* explains, "the essence of matter summed up in the Chinese symbol of Yin and Yang was a symmetry of complementary principles—aptly representing the modern theory of particle-wave duality."

Figure 5.3.

Opposites Are Complementary: The Principle of Mutuality

As I began to consider the implications of the cosmic principle of dynamic balance, I realized that I had already been applying its structure as I went through my own self–transformation. B.T., I had divided all aspects of my world, including myself, into mutually exclusive opposites. But as I began to recognize and accept my

Shadow and then began to create authentically positive alternatives to balance its negative contents, I was in fact creating a system of dynamic balance through the interaction of mutually complementary opposites within my own psyche and my own soul. I now understood that my positive and negative aspects were not mutually exclusive polar opposites. They were *both* part of me. In order to become whole, I had to accept them *both* and keep them balanced.

Intuitively, I had been applying the cosmic principle of dynamic balance and complementarity to my transformation process—and it worked. It worked beyond my wildest expectations. I realized that if I chose to use these concepts consciously, their effects would be even more powerful and far–reaching. I thus developed the first principle of the Balanced Paradigm: **The Principle of Mutuality**.

The universe is created and maintained through the dynamic balance of complementary opposites.
The Principle of Mutuality

The Principle of Mutuality helped me see that in any aspect of life, seeming opposites are not antagonistic, but are mutually complementary. Neither side of an opposition is superior to the other, but instead both sides are important, part of the whole. And contrary to simplistic stereotypes, *each* side of a set of opposites usually contains *both* good *and* bad.

I developed a symbolic diagram to help me visualize the Principle of Mutuality. (See Figure 5.4.)

You will notice that Figure 5.4.—the Principle of Mutuality—changes the vertical orientation of the False Self (Figure 3.1.), turning it horizontally so that the positive and negative sides are not in a hierarchical (I'm good, you're bad) relationship, but in a mutually complementary, equal relationship.

The Principle of Mutuality
"Opposites are mutually complementary."

Figure 5.4.

In figure 5.4., I show the "positive" side with a small negative sign under it and the "negative" side with a small positive sign under it. This is to remind us that neither side is exclusively "all right" or "all wrong," but since opposites are complementary, there is truth on both sides. For simplicity's sake, in future diagrams I will show complementary opposites as "all positive" on one side and "all negative" on the other.

Applying the Principle of Mutuality

I consciously began to apply the Principle of Mutuality to all aspects of my life: to my relationships and interactions with other people, and to how I looked at the world in general.

One of the most important ways in which the Principle of Mutuality improved my life was by increasing my options significantly. Since our belief systems create our reality, if our beliefs tell us we have limited options, our reality *is* limited. For example, take the familiar question: How would you describe this glass? (See Figure 5.5.)

You may say that the glass is half empty. I may say the glass is half full. Who is right and who is wrong? The Principle of Mutuality teaches us the wisdom that we are *both* right. Truth does not exist in mutually exclusive polar opposites, but in dynamic balance between mutually complementary opposites. I can choose to see the glass as *either* half empty *or* half full. An expanded, complementary answer is it is *both*. The bottom half of the glass is filled with water *and* the top half is filled with air. This moves us from a "black–and–white" to a "both/and" perspective.

Figure 5.5.

The benefits of this new perspective are manifold. I have discovered that I can learn from another person whose opinion is different from mine. Instead of seeing the person who disagrees with me as an adversary, he or she has become a teacher, who helps me expand my options and my life.

As we realize that we personally do not have exclusive possession of truth, right, or goodness, we can become more accepting of other people's feelings and points of view. We can also become more open to learning from others' viewpoints in the process of discovering the truth about any issue. We can became better listeners, because we can hear what the other person is saying, rather than having to defend our position. And we can become more open–minded, because we now understand that there is both truth and falsity in any extreme.

Viewing opposites as a necessary, complementary aspect of my life freed me from being attached to one extreme and avoiding another. As the Principle of Mutuality expanded my perceptions, this markedly improved both the effectiveness and quality of my life. I moved from my formerly rigid, categorical way of thinking to a new openness and freedom in both thoughts and actions.

Opposites Are Connected:
The Principle of Association

B. T. , my life had been limited by my belief that everything in the world is separate and isolated. I believed that I was separate from other people, separate from the world around me, and separate from God.

These feelings of isolation were reinforced both by my religious training, which taught me that I was terrible and God was "up there," far away from me and judging me; and also by conventional Newtonian science, which taught that the world was made up of separate pieces of physical matter and that space was dead and empty. These beliefs created painful feelings of loneliness and isolation in me, and at the same time prevented me from trying to build meaningful relationships with other people, since ultimately I did not believe that real relationships were possible.

As I continued to read about the New Science, I discovered that scientists are now theorizing that not only are all aspects of the universe created by dynamic balance between complementary opposites, but in fact, at a deeper level, seeming opposites are actually connected. I discovered numerous examples of the connectedness of seeming opposites.

For example, recent scientific information shows that a

connecting continuum exists in our brains between the electronically positive action state and the electronically negative resting state of our brain cells. (See Figure 5.6.)

Action   **Resting**

Figure 5.6.

Furthermore, although each half of your brain has a distinctly different function, the brain's two hemispheres are interconnected and communicate with each other through a central bundle of nerves, the *corpus callosum*. The connections that exist at deeper levels between seemingly unrelated phenomena can be found everywhere in the universe.

The spectrum is an example of a continuum. When white light is passed through a prism, an entire spectrum, or continuum of different colors appears—violet fading into indigo, which fades into blue, which fades into green...yellow...orange...red.

Einstein's Theory of General Relativity demonstrated that even space and time are not separate. As Fritjof Capra explains, "According to relativity theory, space is not three–dimensional and time is not a separate entity. Both are intimately connected and form a four–dimensional continuum, 'space-time.' In relativity theory, therefore, we can never talk about space without talking about time and vice versa."[22]

Charles Sanders Pierce (1839–1914), considered by many to be America's most distinguished philosopher,

> laughed at the "sheep and goat separators" who split the world into true and false. Rather he held all that exists is continuous, and such

a continuum governs knowledge. For instance, size is a continuum
...time is a continuum, so though an acorn eventually becomes an
oak tree, no one can say exactly when. Speed and weight form
spectrums, as do effort, distance, and intensities of all sorts.
Politeness, anger, joy, and all other feelings and behaviors come in a
continuum. Consciousness itself is a continuum, varying not
only in an individual, from high alertness through a coma, but
also across species, from humans to protozoans.[23]

Mathematicians have recently developed new logic systems
based on the premise that rather than being disconnected, opposites
are actually complementary and connected by a continuum.

In the 1920's the Polish logician Jan Lukasiewicz developed the
principles of multi–valued logic by adding a new category to the
classical Aristotelian logic system. In Aristotelian either/or logic,
the operation of negation defines opposites. For example, if
statement "1" is true, then its opposite, "0" becomes false. But if
statement "1" is false then its opposite, "0" must be true. (See Figure
5.7.)

The Aristotelian Logic System

STATEMENT	NEGATION
1	0
0	1

Figure 5.7.

Lukasiewicz broadened the either/or paradigm by adding a
third value: a half. (See Figure 5.8.)

The implications of Lukasiewicz' invention are revolutionary.
Adding a third number— .5 —demonstrates that we can break out

of a polarized, either/or way of thinking and move to a continuum way of thinking which allows us to deal with the "gray" areas of life. This middle area allows us to respond effectively to seeming certitudes and absolutes, and also makes it possible for us to deal with the numerous paradoxes and ambiguities between the certitudes, which are an inherent part of life.

The Multi-Valued Logic System

STATEMENT	NEGATION
1	0
½	½
0	1

0--------.5 --------1

Figure 5.8.

Multi–valued logic teaches us that what was previously believed to be a void which separated opposites is actually a connecting continuum, which can be measured in degrees of interplay between opposites. This allows for an overlap between apparent opposites, or in other words, it is possible for opposites to have some qualities in common. (See Figure 5.9.)

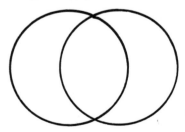

Figure 5.9.

In 1964 Lofti A. Zadeh, then chairman of the Electrical Engineering Department at the University of California, wrote an article titled *"Fuzzy Sets,"* which led to an even newer logic system called "Fuzzy Logic." As *Scientific American* explains, "relations between sets show the paradox at the heart of fuzzy logic. In standard sets, an object either does or does not belong to a set: the glass of water is either empty or full. Fuzzy sets cover a continuum of partial sets, such as the glass is only half full."[24] Fuzzy sets deal with values expressed as degrees rather than discrete numbers.

Aristotelian logic says "It either does or does not." Fuzzy logic has numerous practical applications because it is based on "If... then" propositions and "more or less" assumptions. As a result, fuzzy logic is actually more precise than either/or logic. It is being used to create products such as microwave ovens that watch over meals with precise care, and washing machines that with a single push of a button measure out detergent and choose the correct water temperature. In Japan, a subway system which runs by fuzzy logic is so smooth that when the train stops or starts, you don't even have to hold on to a strap.

Oneness and unity are the only two essential conditions for the new multi–valued logic. *Scientific American* explains, "the only constraint on fuzzy logic is that an object's degrees of membership in complementary groups must sum to unity; if the air seems 20 percent cool, it must also be 80 percent not cool. In this way, fuzzy logic just skirts the bivalent contradiction—that something is 100 percent cool and 100 percent not cool—that would destroy formal logic. The law of the excluded middle holds merely when an object belongs 100 percent to one group." [25] In fuzzy logic, any statement and its opposite must numerically add up to one—which means they are both part of the whole.

These examples helped me to develop the second principle of the

Balanced Paradigm: **The Principle of Association.**

At a deeper level, seeming opposites are connected by a continuum.

The Principle of Association

I also developed a symbolic diagram to help me visualize and apply the Principle of Association. (See Figure 5.10.)

The Principle of Association

Figure 5.10.

Note that in this diagram, not only are the two opposites still horizontal, or complementary, they are also connected by a continuum which contains many different gradations between the two end points. This continuum represents all the varying "shades of gray" between the end points of "black" and "white." Or in real life, it represents the numerous options from which you can choose in any situation.

The Principle of Association allowed me to become aware of the underlying connections which exist between opposites. Previously I believed that opposites were diametrically opposed. The continuum image helps me see that life is actually much more complex. It has also freed me from constantly needing to make judgments, which has helped me let go of prejudices and stereotypes and develop tolerance toward people of opposing views. Instead of feeling comfortable only with others who agree with me, I now accept, enjoy, and learn from people with a whole spectrum of different opinions and behaviors. Since I no longer have to maintain rigid stereotypes and negative projections, my time and energy have been freed up for learning and growing.

The Principle of Association has also helped me deal more effectively with the "gray" areas of life and feel more comfortable facing ambiguity and paradoxes. To me, the many points on the continuum represent the numerous "what if's" of probability thinking rather than the "all or nothing's" or "either/or's" of classic logic. The Principle of Association can provide more information about any situation, which is so essential for making decisions in our increasingly complex world.

Discovering Balanced Thinking

As I continued to apply the Principles of Mutuality and Association and they continued to transform my life, bringing me greater happiness, peace of mind, better personal relationships, and more effectiveness in my professional life, I realized that I was developing a new approach to understanding and acting in the world, which I call "Balanced Thinking."

Balanced Thinking is a process in which:
1. You create an alternative which balances an existing concept, position, or point of view.
2. You envision yourself in the middle of a continuum which connects the two alternatives.
3. You can now look at and choose either end point, or any of the gradations/options from along this continuum.

The diagram in figure 5.11. can help us visualize the process of Balanced Thinking. In figure 5.11., the two opposite alternatives (positive and negative, black and white, etc.) are at the end points of the line, and the line is a continuum with numerous gradations between the two end points. In the middle of the continuum is an "O" which represents the Observer— you or I. Since you are in the middle, you can look at either side, or at any point on the continuum. This allows you to choose from any option along the continuum.

Balanced Thinking

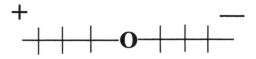

Figure 5.11.

Balance is not a static state, but a dynamic process. Balanced Thinking therefore, is part of a dynamic process of constantly learning, growing, becoming more successful and effective, more compassionate and loving, more spiritually aware, and more at home in the world—always keeping that cosmic sense of humor that the unexpected can happen when you least expect it!

Applying the process of Balanced Thinking in every area of life can help keep us open and vulnerable, at the same time as it helps us become more centered and grounded. It can allow us to integrate head with heart, practical abilities with a mystical awareness; inner depths with everyday, external concerns. Balanced Thinking can help us achieve greater success in both the personal and professional realms, but only if we stay humble even while we are applying and benefitting from our constantly growing gifts and strengths.

Balanced Thinking can help us balance an either/or approach with a wholistic perspective, by balancing analysis and integration, part and whole. It can help us balance our rational thinking abilities and our emotions, our ideas and experiences, our fear of change with an acceptance of change.

Balanced Thinking is a "process" way of thinking. As Erich Jantsch writes in *The Self–Organizing Universe,* "process thinking does not know any sharp separation between the opposite aspects of reality. It also transcends a dialectic synthesis of opposites....In process thinking, there is only the *complementarity* with which opposites include each other."[26] Because Balanced Thinking is a process, it allows us to be aware of the constantly changing nature of reality, and thereby increases our effectiveness in the world. It can also help us realize that there is no such thing as perfection on this planet, since everything is in the process of becoming.

What I am calling "Balanced Thinking" is actually a spiritual discipline. Buddhists call it "the middle way." In the classic book *What the Buddha Taught,* Dr. Walpola Rahula, a Buddhist monk and scholar, writes that the Fourth Noble truth is known as the "Middle Path," because it avoids two extremes: one being the search for happiness through the pleasures of the senses, which is "low, common, unprofitable and the way of ordinary people; the other being the search for happiness through self–mortification in different forms of asceticism, which is painful, unworthy and unprofitable. Having himself first tried these two extremes, and having found them to be useless, the Buddha discovered through personal experiences the Middle Path which gives vision and knowledge, leads to Calmness, Insight, Enlightenment, Nirvana."[27] In *Cutting through Spiritual Materialism,* the Buddhist monk Chogyam Trungpa states that the middle way "is a complete state of being as you are. We could describe this with a lot of words, but one really has to do it. If you really start living the middle way, then you will see it, you will find it. You must allow yourself to trust yourself, to trust in your intelligence. We simply have to let ourselves be."[28]

Chapter 6

Going Deeper and Becoming Whole: The Principle of Centeredness

An Imbalanced Culture

While each of us is also shaped by the larger culture in which we live, we are also distinct individuals, with our own unique gifts, talents, experiences, and purposes in life. This is especially true with regard to our lack of wholeness. The modern Western paradigm in which most of us have grown up is imbalanced in the extreme. It overemphasizes mind over body; head (reason or logic) over heart (emotions or feelings); the left brain over the right brain; the masculine over the feminine; material, external reality over internal, spiritual awareness. In these and many other ways, our culture teaches us to split ourselves in two, to value some parts of ourselves and devalue or even deny other parts. This prevents us from becoming whole.

The belief that we are made up of pairs of disconnected opposites—one pole superior, the other inferior—is reinforced by our tendency to engage in polarized thinking. Therefore, understanding and applying the principles of Mutuality and Association and the process of balanced thinking can help us become more whole. For each pair of "opposites," we need to strengthen or rebuild the devalued or repressed side, then integrate both sides by recognizing their interconnectedness.

In my personal journey I devoted considerable energy to balancing and reintegrating both my masculine and feminine aspects, and my left and right brains. As we look at the emerging new cultural paradigm, we can also see a general shift toward reintegration in both areas.

Integrating Our Masculine and Feminine Aspects

I was conditioned into the prevalent belief that being the "breadwinner" automatically made a man superior. This was based on the assumption that money is the only valid criterion for determining what is of value. And since most women value relationships, this meant that they were inferior.

B.T., I used to live in my head, worshiping reason and logic and disdaining emotions. Having a "cool head," not showing emotions, was also considered a masculine strength, and since women tended to be emotional, this also made them inferior. Beneath my supposed feelings of power and control, I actually felt a tremendous insecurity, because in my heart of hearts I suspected that women might actually be superior because of their effectiveness and determination in relationships.

As I began to value my feminine aspects, emotions became more important and comfortable for me, and I began to appreciate the importance of, and develop genuine, meaningful relationships with both men and women. Because of my competitive spirit B.T., I had plenty of business associates but no true male friends, and I used women primarily to make me look good and to satisfy my sexual needs. A.T., I am concerned about both my own and other people's feelings. Since I no longer feel threatened by other's strengths, I now enjoy treating women with respect, as equal partners, and I have many important and sincere relationships with both men and women.

By accepting both the masculine and feminine aspects of my personality, I no longer fear or deny my emotions, and am now able to experience the richness, color, and texture of an emotional life. Integrating my masculine and feminine sides has allowed me to become a "real man" in the truest sense by combining my expertise in external affairs with an inner discovery of and connection with my inner self, my soul.

Although each of these changes happened to me as an individual, through my own personal work, many cultural commentators have observed that a larger cultural paradigm shift is taking place all around us today, as more and more women are becoming successful in the external world, and more and more men are recognizing the importance of emotions and relationships. This emerging paradigm is not about a new version of dominance or separation, but is a restoration of a long–denied balance between the masculine and feminine aspects of who we are.[30]

Integrating Our Left and Right Brains

Scientists now understand that each of the brain's hemispheres directs a different set of functional abilities.[31] The left half of the brain is in charge of our analytical abilities: our ability to create symbols, to use speech and logic, and to take action. Left–brain functions operate in a linear fashion, enabling us to break down information into separate bits that follow each other along a straight line of reason and one–directional time—from past to present to future. In a sense, the left brain could be called the "masculine" hemisphere.

By contrast, the right half of the brain is wholistic and intuitive, and generates most of our feelings and emotions. It is also the source of our dreams, altered states of consciousness, mystical feelings, and aesthetic appreciation. In a sense, the right brain could be called the "feminine hemisphere."

Although each of the brain's hemispheres has its own distinct set of functions, the two halves are connected by a dense bridge of nerve fibers called the *corpus callosum*, which ensures that the two halves communicate with each other with regard to brain function. To be whole means two things. First, we must honor and value both sides. Second, we must integrate the two sides, the two approaches to life.

Western culture has a long tradition of separating our left from our right brains, and overemphasizing left–brain functions. The idea that emotions should be separate from rationality began with the early Greek philosophers, (such as) Plato and Aristotle. This was later enhanced by an influential motto of the Roman Empire, "*Dux vitae ratio*" which means "logic is the guide of life." Around the beginning of the mechanistic paradigm, when Descartes wrote his famous statement "*Cogito ergo sum*," "I think, therefore I am," he positioned rationality as the only defining criterion of who we are. Cartesian dualism further weakened our acceptance of the belief in a whole brain by creating an imbalanced focus on the left half. As Antonio Damasio writes in *Descartes' Error,* "It was Descartes who not only separated our brains into two, he also was responsible for the separation of reason from emotion...."[32]

However, as part of the emerging paradigm shift, we can see many ways in which both halves are increasingly being valued and integrated. The increasing expansion and blurring of gender roles is one example. Another is the increasing interest in application of mind–body medicine.

Our larger culture is also demonstrating a growing interest in the inner life and emotions, and spiritual practices such as meditation or centering actually increase integration of the brain's two halves. Later in this chapter I describe my own experience with centering, and how it helped me become even more whole.

As each of us takes personal steps to increase our wholeness, we begin to create new cultural beliefs that further inspire and support our desire and ability to change as individuals. Becoming more whole—both as individuals, and by creating a more wholistic cultural paradigm—is yet another example of the transformative process of dynamic balance.

Reclaiming Wholeness

As I applied Balanced Thinking to all areas of my life, formerly divided and discordant parts of myself began to integrate and previously hidden aspects of my being appeared and began to enhance my life. I rediscovered and balanced my positives and negatives, inner spirituality with outer actions, reconnected reason and emotion, mind and body, masculine and feminine aspects, and much more. In other words, I became whole.

Wholeness has many meanings. As we have seen, it is the integrating of opposites. However, reality consists of more than just opposites. It also consists of various parallel but distinct parts which constitute a whole. For example, our bodies are made up of many different organs and organ systems, including the nervous system, the skeletal system, the muscular system, the cardiovascular system, the respiratory system, the gastrointestinal system, and the reproductive system. When each of these systems is healthy and all are working together to insure the health of the person, we can say that person is whole.

Likewise, a human community is made up of many different kinds of people, and an ecosystem is made up of many different kinds of plants, animals, soils, water cycles, etc., each of which must be healthy, and each of which must also communicate or interact with all the other parts of the larger system—be it a human community or ecosystem—in order for that larger system to be healthy and whole.

A familiar description of a whole individual depicts six major areas of life—physical, emotional, social, intellectual, professional, and spiritual—in a pie chart. (See Figure 6.1.)

Aspects of a Whole Person

Figure 6.1.

I was aware of and living only in two of these areas—the professional and the intellectual. Going through my transformation process restored all six parts to my life, making me whole.

With so many parts of myself coming to light and so many opposites being balanced, I developed a new image to visualize what was happening to me. It looked like a wheel with many spokes. Each spoke connects different pairs of seemingly separate but actually interconnected opposites, while the many spaces in between the spokes represent the many other parts and aspects of my life.

The Shape of Wholeness

To celebrate the emergence of increasing wholeness in my life and to help me continue my growth as a whole person, I developed the third principle of the Balanced Paradigm: **The Principle of Wholeness.**

The universe is a coherent whole, made up of countless integrated coherent wholes.

The Principle of Wholeness

I realized that a circle is a natural symbol to help us visualize and support our growth in wholeness.

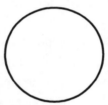

Figure 6.2.

The image of a circle can help us remember our wholeness because it depicts a connection between the downward and upward slopes, left and right sides, in order to create a whole circle. The opposite points on the circle's circumference are complementary and connected, and the circle is also a natural image of process, with one side feeding into the other side, over and over again.

The circle is a basic shape in nature, appearing everywhere: in atoms, spider webs, annual rings of trees, the picture of earth from space, and countless other areas of creation. Circles are also depicted in cultures throughout history. They appear early in Neolithic art, when ancient people engraved "sun wheels" on rocks long before the wheel was even invented. Circles are universally associated with meditation, healing, and prayer. In the Christian tradition they appear as halos around the heads of angels and saints. In the Zen tradition, the circle represents enlightenment. Native Americans used circles in their sand paintings, medicine wheels, and shields, and also created healing circles with groups of people.

Black Elk was a visionary spiritual leader of the Sioux Nation in the late nineteenth century. His book *Black Elk Speaks* even made its way to Europe around the turn of the last century, where it was studied by psychologist Carl Jung and his associates in Vienna.

Black Elk writes:

> Have you ever noticed that everything an Indian does is in a circle, and that is because the Power of the World always works in circles, and everything tries to be round . . .Everything the Power of the World does is done in a circle. The sky is round, and I have been told that the earth is round like a ball, and so are the stars. The wind, in its greatest power, whirls. Birds make their nests in circles, for theirs is the same religion as ours. The sun comes forth and goes down again in a circle. The moon does the same, and both are round. Even the seasons form a great circle in their changing, and always come back again to where they were. The life of a man is a circle from childhood to childhood (in old age), and so it is in everything where power moves. Our tepees were round like the nests of birds, and these were always set in a circle, the nation's hoop, a nest of many nests, where the Great Spirit meant for us to hatch our children.[33]

Whenever I see a full moon, I let its circular imagery remind me of my wholeness. I previously felt incompetent, worthless, valueless—which is represented by the downward slope—but the circle's upward slope reminds me that I also have a corresponding positive side and that I am competent, worthwhile, and of value. The circular image can empower our self–actualization process by helping us recognize that we already possess a wholistic perspective.

Seeking the Center

To become whole is a wonderful experience—but it can also be overwhelming. As I became more whole, I become aware of a joyful, ecstatic profusion of diversity and interconnectedness—inward to myself, outward to other people and to the whole Earth and all its beings, and outward farther to the larger universe. To become whole means to break through so many limits and live with vastly expanded openness and awareness. In the midst of so many interconnections and so many choices, how can you stay centered, focused, balanced and in touch with the right direction in your life? The answer is that you must balance the exuberant glories of wholeness with the focused inner stillness of centering.

I first heard about "centering" at the Harvard Divinity School. Centering is regularly practiced in Eastern religious and spiritual traditions and has also been used by Christian spiritual explorers. Eastern traditions usually call this process "meditation," while Christians call it "contemplation."

My studies explained that meditation/centering brings greater balance to life in two ways: it puts you in touch with a calm, inner center of balance in the midst of life's external turmoil; and it helps you connect to your inmost spiritual core while at the same time opening you up to a higher, cosmic level of consciousness. *The Random House Encyclopedia* describes the phenomena of centering as follows:

There are five levels of consciousness generally associated with meditation [centering]....At the first level the body is relaxed and the mind stilled. Ordinary wakefulness is then transcended by a state of deep rest but alertness in which the mind is more intensely aware of itself. This state of personal consciousness is transcended by cosmic consciousness, a sense of illumination beyond the boundaries of self and time. The next stage is God consciousness, or the inseparability of creator and creation. Finally, at the highest level of all, consciousness itself is transcended in a unity with the whole or oneness. [34]

After learning all this I was filled with an intense desire to experience centering. However, I did not want to practice it as part of some specific religion. I wanted to experience centering directly, without all the trappings of a dogmatic religion. In addition to its spiritual aspects, I learned that centering also helps mobilize our body's inner resources, helping heal physical and emotional disease, inducing greater relaxation, and helping reduce depression, irritability, and stress disorders. The Mind/Body Workbook for cancer patients from a Harvard Medical teaching hospital explains that "when thoughts become focused as desires (attractions and aversions) and it is inappropriate to take action, our muscles begin to tense up and our anxiety increases. When in the process of meditation we let go of desires by adopting an attitude of nonattachment to those thoughts, then we are able to relax."[35] Further readings about spiritual approaches to and health–related applications of meditation or centering introduced me to a variety of pragmatic techniques through which I learned how to practice centering. [36]

After practicing centering and experiencing its results, I

developed the fourth principle of the Balanced Paradigm: **The Principle of Centeredness**.

> Each of us has an original inner core, or Center of Balance,
> which is the key to our authentic self and inherent spirituality.
> **The Principle of Centeredness**

I also discovered several symbolic images which can help us visualize our center, in relation to both our individual self and the larger external world.

One image that I use is a circle with a point inside, at its center. The point symbolizes the integrative center of your being, from which you can be aware of, yet remain unattached to, the various aspects of your life, while the larger circle represents your inherent wholeness. (See Figure 6.3.)

Figure 6.3.

Another image which can help you visualize your original center is a candle. The candle represents your wholeness, while the wick running up and down through the middle of the candle represents your original Center of Balance. (See Figure 6.4.)

Figure 6.4.

Also an image of your center is the axle of a wheel; the wheel turns, but its center stays in the same place. (See Figure 6.5.)

Figure 6.5.

Yet another visual representation of your center is the Eastern Yantra. The images depict a central point surrounded by two complementary triangles, one upright, the other inverted. (See Figure 6.6.)

Figure 6.6.

In *Man and His Symbols*, Carl Jung wrote that "in terms of psychological symbolism [yantras] express the union of opposites—the union of the personal temporal world of the ego with the nonpersonal, timeless world of the non–ego. Ultimately, this union is the fulfillment and goal of all religions."[37] He also wrote that "the center symbolizes the perfect state where masculine and feminine are united. The world of illusions has finally vanished. All energy has gathered together in the initial state...it shows then, the union of all opposites, and is embedded between yin and yang, heaven and earth, the state of everlasting balance."[38]

The Experience of Centering

I chose one centering technique and began to practice it for 20 minutes each day. At first I didn't feel I was "getting it." Either my mind continued to chatter while I tried to center, or else I became very drowsy. (I later learned that these experiences are common to many people when they first try to center.) I was determined to master the experience. I realized that my major distraction was wondering when the 20 minutes were going to be up, so I set a timer for 20 minutes and continued the practice. After about a month I was able to clear my mind, the sleepiness went away, and I began to feel present in the moment. I was getting it!

The daily centering practice slowly began to affect the rest of my life, helping me feel more grounded and aware throughout the day. After I had been doing it steadily every day for a few months, I began to slack off due to time constraints. Sometimes I did not have 20 minutes to just sit down quietly and center. However, on those days that I did not center, I felt off balance, less calm, and more easily agitated. I was also more likely to fall back into addictive behaviors. This proved to me that centering was really having an effect, so I made a commitment to myself to center every day from then on.

Gradually the practice of centering reached out to transform more and more of my life. Whenever I emerged from my 20 minutes of centering, I began to feel in touch with my inner being, felt better about myself, and more connected with the larger cosmos. I began to get a sense of being in touch with my original center—a spiritual sense that I was innately a good person, a blessed child of the universe, worthy of love and able to love others.

Once I began to experience my original center, I developed a heartfelt, genuine approach to life. My natural curiosity was unleashed and I wanted to learn about everything around me, since everything is part of the moment–to–moment unfolding of creation. Also I increasingly wanted to rid myself of the unnecessary mental and emotional "baggage" I had been carrying around, deluding myself that it would somehow make me happy. My entire life had been spent chasing things, while totally forgetting who I really was.

Becoming centered helped transform my volatile temperament. B.T., I used to live on an emotional roller coaster, always feeling extremes of being either really up or really down. As I became more centered, I developed an even temperament for the first time in my life. I stopped over–reacting to people, and became able to find something funny in stressful situations or able to realize that some things are simply not worth getting upset over. Not only has centering helped free me from inner conflicts, but my inner peace further contributes to peace in the larger sphere of life, in my relationships with family, friends, colleagues, and the world in general.

As centering helped me move my mental activity away from an exclusive focus on the external details of everyday existence, my awareness reconnected to both deeper and higher levels of consciousness. Centering provided the space for my inner meaning to emerge. I began to realize that we are all here on this planet—alive today—for a reason. It is the job of each of us to work with the creative process to discover what our purposes are, and to fulfill them in the time each of us has remaining.

Centering helps me stay in touch with what is important, with who I really am. Even though it has had such a powerful impact, however, I remember that life is dynamic. Some days I feel more connected to my inner core and other days I feel disconnected; some days I feel really good about myself and others I don't. The big difference is that now when I am "off center," I am not far from my original core, and I know what to do to bring myself back.

Spiritual Aspects of Centering

I believe that each of us has a Center of Balance—the center of pure awareness with which we were naturally born. I experienced this pure awareness the night my son Justin came into the world. After 12 hours of labor, the doctor decided to perform a Caesarean section on Judy. After the procedure the head nurse asked if I would take Justin into the next room while they finished attending to Judy.

In a dimly lit Recovery Room at three o'clock in the morning, this newborn child stared into my eyes with an awareness that I will never forget. I heard myself asking him the following questions which emerged from the depths of my being: "What do you already know? Where did you come from?" I then heard myself say, "Welcome to the world of experience. In your life you will have 'good' and 'bad' experiences, but it is only through having both experiences that you will grow." At the moment I felt connected with the essence of creation.

I have learned that centering can help us enter, hear, and attune to the wisdom that exists deep within our beings. The time you spend listening to your silent voice of wisdom can be empowering and spiritually fulfilling.

Paradoxically, connecting with this deep, essential self also helped me become aware of my inherent connection with the whole of creation. Centering opened a channel which allowed me to make a connection with the largest whole—the universe itself. Figure 6.7 symbolically depicts our connection to the web of creation throughout the universe, by showing a series of ripples made after a rock has been thrown into a pool of water. The inner ripple is your original core. The next ripple out is your individual life, the next ripple represents your personal circle of relationships, the next ripple is our larger society, the next is our planet, then out to our solar system, to our Milky Way galaxy, to the local group of galaxies, and on out to the largest ripple, the universe itself. (See Figure 6.7.)

Centering helped me realize that the creative life force of the universe has loved me enough to have created me, that each day is

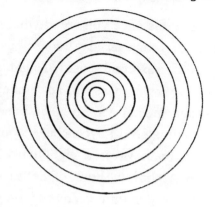

Figure 6.7.

a new paragraph in the book of creation, and my life—and the lives of every one of us—are an integral part of this story.

How to Center

The different centering techniques all have the same goal—to slow down your brain's electrical activity by focusing your awareness. This is especially important in our culture, where we are constantly bombarded by sights and sounds. (Just think how many times a day you are exposed to advertisements, all screaming for your attention.)

In order to practice centering, it helps to understand how your brain waves function. The electrical activity in your brain is yet another example of dynamic balance, since your brain cycles are created by complementary opposites, a high and a low, as illustrated in Figure 6.8.

Beta

Alpha

Figure 6.8.

When you are reading this page you are at what is called beta level, the mental level of your everyday consciousness. At this stage you are using your five external senses of sight, sound, smell, taste and touch, and your brain is in an analytical mode, characterized by constant mental activity. The beta level of our brain functions at approximately 14 cycles per second.

The next level of your brain waves, at eight to twelve cycles per second, is the alpha level. Alpha is the home of the "sub–conscious," characterized by creativity and intuition. You experience your alpha level when you are just ready to fall asleep at night or when you first wake up in the morning.

Have you ever noticed how, despite your greatest intentions to change, your New Year's resolutions usually fail after a short time? This is because you made a conscious decision to change at the beta level, yet the source of your habits actually resides in alpha, so you have to change the "program" which exists in your alpha level before lasting change can occur. This can be done through centering and visualization, which is why so many creative and successful people use visualization in order to achieve their goals. (See Chapter 2, the section on visualization.)

Centering slows down your brain's electrical waves. Most of us are in alpha cycle only when we first wake up in the morning and the last moment when we fall asleep at night; the rest of the day you are probably in your beta cycle, the brain level of "doing." So give yourself an "awareness break" by regularly connecting with your inner self for twenty minutes a day. This allows you to create a new pattern which brings greater balance between "doing" and "being" throughout the day. (See Figures 6.9 and 6.10.)

Typical Brain Wave Pattern

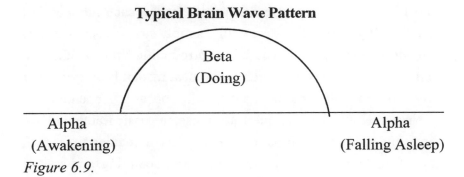

Figure 6.9.

A More Effective and Balanced Brain Wave Pattern

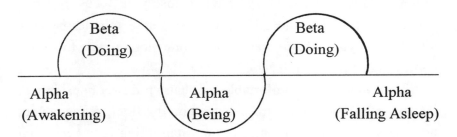

Figure 6.10.

The Balanced Centering Technique

After reading numerous books on Zen meditation and medically–recommended relaxation techniques, I developed the Balanced Centering Technique which utilizes the principle of complementarity and the balanced rhythm of breathing to lower mental activity level from beta to alpha. Because I am extremely visually oriented, I needed a visual focus to help me center. Some techniques suggest that you count downward from "ten" to "one," but I needed even more time to slow down my thinking, which is why I came up with the technique of circling each number as I breathed. If you find this distracting, simply say or visualize each number internally, without adding a surrounding circle. Additional centering techniques, in which you repeat a sound, observe your stream of thoughts, or look at a mandala, appear in Appendix B.

No matter which technique you choose, the basic framework for centering is always the same. First, select a regular time each day—for 20 minutes every day—to practice centering, and make a commitment to center for this period every day, even if you do not feel like it. Find a quiet place, free of noise or other distractions. Set a timer, such as your watch or the timer on a microwave, for 19 minutes. This way you do not have to lose your focus by being concerned about time. (You set the timer for 19 minutes because after it rings you will still need at least one more minute to slowly come out of the centered state.)

Sit on whatever is comfortable—a chair, pillow, or cushion, or if you prefer, you can sit cross–legged on the floor. Arrange your body in an upright position. The important thing is to keep your back straight since you are assuming a regal position (which is your natural birthright); this allows your energy to flow freely through your body. Place your hands on the tops of your thighs, or together in a praying position.

Now begin to breathe slowly, evenly, and deeply. While focusing your consciousness on breathing slowly in and out, visualize the number "10." Visualize enclosing that number within a circle in the following manner: as you slowly breathe in, create the downward curve of the circle, and as you slowly breathe out, create the upward half of the circle. Once the number is circled, if you like you can focus on it while taking a few slow, deep breaths in and out.

When you are ready, breathe in and visualize a straight line descending downward, then visualize the number "9," and then breathe out. Again, create a circle around the number "9" by first breathing in, creating a downward side to the enclosing circle, then breathing out and creating an upward side to the circle.(If your mind wanders, simply repeat the encircling process and stay on the number at which your awareness became distracted until your focus returns.) When you are ready, slowly breathe in, visualize a downward line, then visualize the number "8" and breathe out. Continue this process of visualizing descending numbers and moving down until you reach zero. (See Figure 6.11.) Stay at this level, slowly breathing in and breathing out, and experience the silence of the moment. Silence is the language of your soul; it provides you with a balance to the never–ending flow of stimuli in this Information Age, and creates a connection between your soul and the larger creation, since silence is also the voice of the divine creative force of the universe.

If your mind wanders while you are at zero, refocus your awareness on your slow breathing in and out. Continue to experience the calmness and stillness until the timer rings.

Now it is time to return to beta, your everyday consciousness. Take another minute to reverse the process, by slowly breathing in and out while moving your awareness from "1" back up to "10." (See Figure 6.12.) Imagine that you are returning to the surface during a scuba dive. You need to come up slowly in order not to get the "mental bends." As you exhale, visualize starting from "1," and encircle it while breathing in and out. Then move up to "2" and continue this process until you reach your beta level at the number "10." Once you arrive at "10," open your eyes.

The Balanced Centering Technique

<u>Breathe In</u>   <u>Breathe Out</u>

(10)

↓

(9)

↓

(8)

↓

(7)

↓

(6)

↓

(5)

↓

(4)

↓

(3)

↓

(2)

↓

(1)

↓

0

Figure 6.11 .

Coming out of the Balanced Centering Technique

<u>Breathe In</u>   <u>Breathe Out</u>

(10)

↑

(9)

↑

(8)

↑

(7)

↑

(6)

↑

(5)

↑

(4)

↑

(3)

↑

(2)

↑

(1)

↑

0

Figure 6.12.

Centering Anytime, Anywhere

After you have practiced centering on a regular basis, you can quickly center yourself at any time during the day when you feel the need to become calm and want to step back from a stressful situation. Here are a few techniques that I use to center myself anytime, anywhere. You can imagine a line which runs up and down through the middle of your body. Focus your awareness on this centering line. Another simple way to center yourself at any time is to visualize a circle, which represents your life's wholeness, and see yourself centered in the middle of that circle. A third simple method is to choose a small, special object such as a stone or crystal which you can carry in your pocket. Every time you feel your special object, let it remind you of your inner core and your connection to the larger universe.

These and the other Centering Techniques described in Appendix B allow you to tap into the deep source of creativity and wisdom that already exist within you, just waiting to be discovered. By reconnecting with your inner core through the Centering Techniques, you allow the "unconscious competence" which resides in alpha to flow into the rest of your life.

Since there is no "magic pill" for making transformational changes in your life, you need to regularly participate in doing your own inner work. This is especially true with centering. The rest of your day is probably focused on the external, with no time for your inner self. You deserve to take the time to allow your internal essence to emerge. In the creation of any friendship, you need to spend time with the other person. It is only by taking the time to center yourself on a daily basis that you begin to restore a direct, intimate relationship with your own original core.

Chapter 7

Staying on Course Through Life's Ups and Downs: The Principle of Dynamic Reversal

My goal A.T. has been to connect with and express my inner being and spirituality and live my life's mission to the fullest. That is *my* responsibility. Since I no longer try to control the world around me, this means that life is full of surprises, both positive and negative.

It would be unrealistic to say that negative experiences will never happen or that what you perceive as "bad" will not happen again. Even when we are trying to live with integrity, seeking to have a more positive impact on the world around us, we still cannot control everything that happens. We will never be "perfect," and there is always more to learn. Rather than viewing your life's circumstances and events judgmentally, it is far more productive to use them as lessons for your growth. In fact, some of the greatest lessons that we can learn often evolve from "bad" experiences. It is important to learn how to stay calm and positive in the flow of life, and to develop a balanced mental attitude which helps turn the negative surprises that life brings into positives.

As I explained in the previous chapter, each of us has within ourselves a center of wisdom and universal connectedness which we can experience through centering practices. After becoming familiar with the experience of my deep inner center, I was able to use this experience to help me stay centered through life's positive and negative surprises. This helped me develop the fifth principle of the Balanced Paradigm: **The Principle of Dynamic Reversal**.

> The universe is a constant flow of ever–changing reality, to which we can respond creatively.
>
> **The Principle of Dynamic Reversal**

The Visual Image of Dynamic Balance

Another way of expressing the Principle of Dynamic Reversal is that you are able to stay centered and connected to your deepest inner wisdom through the course of life's ups and downs. A visual image of life's ups and downs is the sine wave. (See Figure 7.1.) As it rises and falls over and over, the sine wave visually depicts the process of dynamic balance, which occurs everywhere throughout the universe.

The Sine Wave:
A Visual Representation of Dynamic Balance

Figure 7.1.

In order to create a visual image of how centering allows you to stay balanced through the course of life's constantly changing flow, I turned the sine wave into its vertical position, and drew a vertical line, which rises straight up through the zigzags of life, as a symbolic representation of this calm inner center. (See Figure 7.2.) I use this image to remind me of the Principle of Dynamic Reversal.

The Principle of Dynamic Reversal

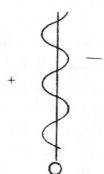

Figure 7.2.

The imagery of Dynamic Reversal mirrors the universal process of dynamic balance. (See Chapters 4 and 5.) Because you now understand that opposites are not mutually exclusive absolutes, but are complements which are inherently connected, this enables you to see the positives in the negatives and the negatives in the positives, and provides you with the ability to transform any negative into a positive.

Dynamic Reversal allows us to turn our negative experiences into positive ones, even when everything seems to be going wrong. It helps us have a positive attitude in negative situations which is essential, since your attitude is your "mind's paintbrush," with which you can "color any situation" no matter what happens. Your attitude is one thing in life that you can control.

Examples of Dynamic Reversal

I have used the Principle of Dynamic Reversal constantly in both my work and personal lives, and have actively taught and shared it with others through the message, "We can turn the negative events in our lives into positives." This practice has enhanced both my life and the lives of the people around me, and their use of it has inspired me even further.

Dynamic Reversal helped me when I started Designer Orthopedics. For an entrepreneur, there is no distinction between your personal and professional lives, because when you start a company, home life and work become one. To be successful in business you need many things, but the fundamental need is for capital, especially as you grow, since growth consumes money—for inventory, increased payrolls, and accounts receivable. As I continually put my own money into the company to keep it going, the Principle of Dynamic Reversal helped me stay positive, centered and trusting through the hell of going from "nouveau riche" to "nouveau poor."

Dynamic Reversal also helped after the fiery destruction of my company's main supplier. I had just flown into Chicago, where I was to give a sales presentation to a major orthopedic distributor. The next day I was going to drive out to our main supplier in Warsaw, Indiana to meet with the company president, since he wanted to turn all sales and marketing efforts over to us, which would allow him to focus on his company's manufacturing strength. A few minutes before I was to give a three–hour presentation to the distributor's entire sales force, I got a phone call from my office in Boston. My secretary had just heard from the president of the Warsaw manufacturing company who informed her that it was a waste of time for me to come to their plant since it had burnt down the previous night.

We had just lost our major supplier of products. To distance myself from my almost overwhelming feelings of shock and fear, I took a few deep breaths to calm myself down. This allowed me to move back to my deep inner sense of awareness. I decided then and there that my company was not going out of business. Somehow we would find another supplier. With this sense of assurance, I then went into the conference room and gave the distributor's sales force a powerful motivational and educational seminar on our product line. No one there knew what had just happened.

When I entered my corporate offices in Boston the next morning, people there were stunned and crying. I brought everyone into our meeting room and drew the Dynamic Reversal image on the blackboard. I told them that in this time of crisis, our attitudes—not the fire—would determine our company's success or failure. My people needed to clear their minds of the fear of losing their jobs, so we could go ahead and explore calmly, clearly, and positively what our options were. And in fact, we quickly found another supplier while the company in Warsaw recovered from the fire.

Then there is the "Saga of Norman White." This should fall under the category of fiction, but it actually happened. After Designer Orthopedics was in operation for two years, it was doing well and growing, with an excellent staff and distribution network, but we still had cash flow problems and some difficulty in obtaining products at the volume that we needed. At a social gathering I met Dr. Norman White. He had earned two doctorates—one from MIT and the other as a cardiologist—and told me he was now practicing at Massachusetts General Hospital. We became friends and after a few months he said that he wanted to invest in my company. He also said that he could provide manufacturing for some of my company's product line, where we were having procuring problems.

I visited the manufacturing company near Boston where Dr. White was a majority owner, and their General Manager assured me that they could easily make our product line. Norman then invested $15,000 in Designer Orthopedics and attended a stockholders' meeting where he met my company's 16 other surgeon–investors. He then wrote a check for $120,000 for new manufacturing equipment, so his company could make our products. Shortly thereafter his accountant began to work part–time in my office.

Norman and I took several trips together throughout the Midwest, visiting my other suppliers. We went to Las Vegas to work my company's exhibition booth at the American Academy of Orthopedic Surgeon's National Convention, and as the convention was ending, my office manager phoned me from Boston to tell me that Norman had called her regularly and asked how much she had deposited into my company's checking account each day.

Troubled by this, I checked our bank records as soon as I returned to Boston, and discovered that $10,000 was missing. I was even more stunned to find that the withdrawal slips had been signed by Norman's accountant who had been working in my office. This was a significant blow to my company, because I was counting on this money to pay off our vendors. In a state of shock, because he was both a friend and an investor, I called Norman White to my office. When he arrived, I confronted him with the fact that $10,000 was missing. He said he had to go to the men's room, walked out of my office—and I never saw him again.

A week later I received an astounding letter from him. He would not only pay back the $10,000, but he offered to assume the entire debt of Designer Orthopedics, for which he wanted 90 % control of the company. At that moment I decided that I would never let him take over my company. I realized that his ultimate goal was to use the company as a vehicle to defraud doctor–investors on a national basis, and I was determined to stop him.

I hired a private investigator, who after a few weeks reported that "Dr. Norman Gray" was no doctor, and presented pages upon pages of his history of fraud and deceit in the Boston area. After he left Boston, we discovered that he had embezzled $40,000 from a medical manufacturing company in North Carolina. I worked with detectives from five local towns, two district attorneys in Boston and a District Attorney's office in North Carolina, and was instrumental in convicting Norman White for the first time. The judge made him pay retribution for his embezzlement from my company and sentenced him to a year in jail.

Norman White was a pathological liar who totally lacked human feelings. What he did was copy values and emotions from other people and then reflected them back, since he was completely empty inside. He had deceived many intelligent people, including real surgeons and very successful businesspeople. He was fully aware that I had personally risked the roof over my head for Designer Orthopedics, yet he stole the $10,000 so that he could push my company over the edge and take it over.

Norman White's web of ruthless, manipulative scheming had seriously endangered my company and me; I was at first so deeply emotionally wounded that it was hard to restore my trust in anyone. The Principle of Dynamic Reversal enabled me to deal with this incredible saga of deceit and betrayal. Realizing what this experience had done to me, I knew that I had to move beyond my negative reaction. I had the power within myself to choose how I would respond. If I stayed negative and untrusting, it would hurt both the company and me, not only in the present but also in the future. I practiced centering continually, which allowed me to fully experience all the hurt I felt from being used. I then chose the positive course by pulling Designer Orthopedics out of debt and moved us forward to national success.

Applying the Principle of Dynamic Reversal

You cannot control what happens to you in life, but by being centered you are able to step back from what is happening in the moment, and not get caught up in reacting to it. This allows you to reflect on the broader process of life, remembering the Principle of Dynamic Reversal and its visual image, which reminds you that positives and negatives continually flow one into the other. The Principle of Dynamic Reversal allows you to choose the one thing you can control—your attitude—which allows you to look for and act on the positive in the negative, or at the very least, to transform negative situations into positive learning experiences. The Chinese language expresses this concept, since the Chinese word for "crisis" also means "opportunity," or as a popular saying goes, "When life gives you lemons, make lemonade."

I have taught everyone close to me to respond to the cyclical, ever–changing nature of life with the Principle of Dynamic Reversal. There are going to be good times as well as bad times; but each of us has the power to choose our attitude, find the positive in the negative, and learn the lessons we need for our personal growth.

I asked my daughter Amy to write about how the Principle of Dynamic Reversal has influenced her life. She provided the following three examples. First, "During my entire life I have attempted to draw the good from my parents' divorce. From both parents' families, there are unique and valuable qualities that can be appreciated. Rather than dwelling on the negative, I have chosen to try to appreciate the best in the situation. Much of my outlook came from you [Dad] always focusing on the positive while I was growing up." Second, "Before my surgery in Atlanta you had given the advice that I could not control the situation, I could only control my reaction to it. This realization allowed me to give up control and I reacted positively during adversity. My surgery was a success and I had peace of mind during the course of the day." Her third example of finding the positive in a negative situation was "when Robert [the man she was dating, who later became her husband] and I separated, "I tried to remain positive and gather the lessons from the hurtful experience. I realized that without experiencing true loneliness, one cannot experience true togetherness. This time in my life was one of the most difficult. Although I would not want to relive this period in my life, it did prove that our internal strength is very powerful."

I can apply the wisdom of Dynamic Reversal to appreciating my parents. Although they conditioned me into many negative assumptions and beliefs, they also taught me a good value system. I attribute my strong work ethic and concern for justice and equality directly to them.

Dynamic Reversal can give us the freedom to know that it is OK to make mistakes, since mistakes are part of life's learning process. We can learn from Nancy Kerrigan, the United States Olympic figure skating silver medal winner. She overcame a debilitating anxiety disorder, expressed in a tide of self–doubt that would overwhelm her whenever she made a mistake on the ice. She explained, "I turned a lot of negative thoughts into positive ones. Instead of making a mistake on the ice and saying to myself, Oh you stink! I learned to just leave the negative thoughts behind and focus on one thing at a time instead of letting a mistake follow me through a performance."

A judgmental, critical upbringing may have made it hard for us to view our mistakes as part of a continuous learning process. But like Nancy Kerrigan, we can remember that even our mistakes have a positive side. Learning from our mistakes is a key to our personal growth, and the Principle of Dynamic Reversal can provide us with the ability to view every situation as a learning experience, rather than judging it as either good or bad.

As you practice the Principle of Dynamic Reversal, you gain three benefits. First, you gain equanimity, a calmer response to life, rather than being overwhelmed by and over–reacting to negative events. Second, the Principle of Dynamic Reversal can help provide you with the inner confidence of knowing that you can handle any situation that arises, since no matter what happens, you have the ability within yourself to find the hidden advantage in any negative situation. This enhances your faith in yourself and makes it easier to accept change. Third, the imagery of Dynamic Reversal can help you develop a basic trust in the flow of your life. Dynamic Reversal reminds you that even though things may seem negative at the time, they are inherently connected to the positive evolutionary growth in your life, an insight which allows you to ride the wave of life, instead of fighting it.

By accepting both the negative and positive aspects of life, you become a whole person. The wholistic view of the Principle of Dynamic Reversal allows you to see negative events from a larger, dynamic, creative perspective. When everything is going well, enjoy the positive, but also be aware of the ever changing flow of life. Remember that you have the ability to minimize the negative and maximize the positive in any situation.

Changing Your Attitude as a Positive Act

In some negative circumstances there may be nothing you can do except maintain a positive attitude, no matter what. Even this can have a positive impact, since your choice of attitude can help other people expand the way they see the world. My wife Judy demonstrated this point in the following letter which she wrote to her colleagues at Eastern Airlines when she knew she was facing her death.

A Special Message

TWU-AFL-CIO   March 1988

Dear Fellow Flight Attendants,

Some of you know me, some of you I have met briefly and some of you I've yet to meet, but I'd like to share my thoughts with all of you.

I have been told that my cancer has worsened and that short of a miracle I may not have long to live. Many thoughts have come and gone since I was told that I have cancer. Trying to face the possibility of death I have looked for meaning in my life and have tried to see what my 15 years as a flight attendant mean to me.

I started as most of us did with the idea of working and traveling for a few years and then getting another job. Why do we stay? The poet in me tells of being able to work where the ancient gods played and the artist in me remembers the spectacular sunrises and sunsets that I have seen. I have seen the sun on cloudy days. I have seen more stars than any earthbound person. The only people who travel higher than us are the astronauts. We have seen that this land has no boundaries, no lines to separate. Countries, states, counties or towns can be seen from 35,000 feet.

We also took this job, because we said we liked people. I have found a family in my coworkers. I have found people to laugh with, people to care about and people to be with. There are the gatekeepers in cities distant from my home who have always brightened my day when they opened the airplane door. I'll always remember the special crews who made working on holidays fun.

I have looked at the purpose that we serve in this hectic world. We all need people, we need smiles, kind words and the ability to sense a problem. In this job we are blessed with being able to give as well as receive. Our thoughtfulness and caring are our strongest assets. I have helped when others needed it and now I am on the receiving end and I can attest to how terrific your love and care feels to receive. You have made Christmas continue through February. Your cards and calls and financial help have given me strength and laughter when I've needed it most.

We live and work in a technological and increasingly sterile world where greed is close to becoming god, but we must remember that most of our passengers are just as afraid of corporate takeovers and layoffs as we are. We must learn to care for and love our brothers or we could lose the whole human race. We are in a unique position to use our strengths to help the world change. We see most of the people who think they run this country every day. We can humanize them, we can show them how to care for strangers and friends. We can make this job meaningful every day and we can change the world.

Keep smiling, keep caring, keep loving and enjoy your life every day. May peace and love find a home in your heart. I hope that miracles do happen and that I'll join you back on the line soon.

Judy Ahrens–Beauregard

Chapter 8

Allowing Miracles to Happen: The Principle of Universal Connectedness

Healing the Split Between Science and Religion

Until recently, Western society has seen a growing conflict between religion and science. During most of the last 400 years, the developments of modern astronomy, geology, and biology led to two increasingly antagonistic world views. Religious doctrines, based on Scripture, taught that the earth, which is the center of the universe, was created 6,000 years ago, and humanity, uniquely made in God's image, was God's highest creation. Meanwhile, science was discovering that the earth is merely one of many planets which revolve around our sun; that ours is only one of many solar systems; that our planet is over 4 billion years old; and that we humans evolved about 3 million years ago from less intelligent primates.

This split between science and religion grew even more extreme during this century, with the popularity of the reductionist approach, which asserts that all phenomena can be understood in terms of the characteristics of their smallest building blocks. As this perspective was expanded to all areas of life, including human interactions and personality, we were told that "according to science," what we think of as consciousness, intelligence, feelings, emotions, and even spiritual experiences are merely the results of chains of molecular and chemical interactions; and that there is no larger spirit or design in the universe, but everything in the world emerged purely as the result of chance, the random interaction of molecules. From this assertion it was only a short jump to the conclusion that human beings are inherently selfish and materialistic, without grandeur or dignity, and that religious beliefs and spiritual experiences are merely illusions.

In recent years the paradigm has again begun to shift, as the discoveries of the New Science have once again revolutionized our understanding of the history of the universe, the nature of life, and humanity's role in the cosmos. During the past 50 years, serious scientists have shown an increasing eagerness to explore the spiritual implications of the New Science and show how their discoveries are compatible with a deeply spiritual view of the world and of life. Even Einstein himself said that "science without religion is lame; religion without science blind."

In recent years, some of the books written by physicists, biologists, and other scientists which seek to integrate science and spirituality include: Robert M. Augros and George N. Stanciu, *The New Story of Science*; Fritjof Capra, *The Tao of Physics*; Jean Charon, *The Unknown Spirit*; Paul Davies, *God and the New Physics*; Timothy Ferris, *The Whole Shebang;* Arthur Peacocke, *God and the New Biology;* Menas Kafatos and Robert Nadeau, *The Conscious Universe;* Brian Swimme, *The Hidden Heart of the Cosmos;* and Fred Alan Wolf, *The Spiritual Universe.*

Meanwhile, modern theologians such as Teilhard de Chardin, Thomas Berry, Matthew Fox, Ramon de Mendoza, and many others have been exploring how the New Science can offer us a transformed approach to religion, in which human beings—aware of the awesome grandeur of a 15–billion–year old, continually evolving universe—can actively participate as conscious, responsible, and loving co–participants in its evolution. Of special interest is the work of Thomas Berry and other thinkers influenced by him, especially the mathematical cosmologist Brian Swimme. As they seek to integrate the discoveries of the New Science with a religious and spiritual perspective, they talk about "the new Creation Story," an expanded vision of the universe and humanity's place in it, which emphasizes both our connection to the evolving universe and in particular to this planet, and our obligation to care for all life on earth.[40]

Some of the scientists and theologians listed above are trying to integrate the New Science with Christianity or the Western conception of an anthropomorphic God; some try to show that it is compatible with Hinduism or other Eastern religions or spiritual philosophies; and some seek to redefine our conception of God and spirituality in the light of the new scientific findings.

Religion, Science, and a Mystical Spirituality

I personally make a distinction between "religion" and "spirituality." I believe that the many religions of the world were founded as diverse expressions of spirituality, so each religion has its own particular doctrines and practices. But as scholars of religion have recently been learning and mystics throughout history have experienced directly, there are basic teachings which underlie all religions. For example, the universe is filled with spirit; our purpose here on earth is to connect with the divine, discover and fulfill our unique personal mission, and express love and compassion for all beings; and ultimately we are all interconnected, we are all one. By "spirituality" I am talking about the universal principles which underlie all religions, and which have the potential to unite humankind in the spirit of respect and love.

Like the mystics of old, I too have personally experienced the reality of these spiritual truths. On several occasions I have had a direct, mystical experience of the divinity of the universe, losing for the moment my sense of myself as an individual, and experiencing my connection to the oneness of the universe. Furthermore, I do not consider these experiences supernatural or unusual. I believe they reflect the way our lives are meant to work once we realize we are part of a living, interconnected, purposeful universe. In fact, studies have shown that almost one out of ten people has undergone a genuinely mystical experience, emerging full of trust in the larger reality. Most people, however, do not tell others about these experiences for fear of being called "weird" or "crazy." Who knows how many more of us have experienced this sense of oneness and universal connectedness, but have been afraid to talk about it openly?

Mystical spirituality is a valid spiritual tradition, and many scientists today are observing that the latest discoveries in their fields about the nature of life and the universe actually validate and support the perceptions of mystics. The following sections describe two major conclusions of the New Science which correlate with the experiences of mystical spirituality: the proposition that the universe is interconnected—we are all one; and that the evolving universe is filled with intelligence, directed by a "cosmic mind" in which each of us participates.

All Parts of the Universe Are Interconnected

The latest discoveries and theories about the origin and evolution of our universe demonstrate that we all share the same physical origins. Contemporary cosmology began in 1929, when astronomer Edwin Hubble discovered that galaxies are traveling away from each other and the universe is expanding, or in other words, that the universe is not static, but is still evolving and changing.

Most scientists today believe the universe and everything in it came into being approximately 15 billion years ago with the explosion of a cosmic fireball, or "Big Bang." You and I and everything else in the world—all the energy, space, and time that make up our past, present, and future—were created in that moment in time. However, the universe was not created in its present form instantaneously. Its components have continued to develop and evolve over billions of years, and this creative process is still taking place. The recent discoveries made possible by the new Hubble space telescope have shown us the "nurseries" where at this very moment new stars are being born.

Yet everything in this universe, past, present, and future, from atoms to human beings to stars, came from the explosion of that cosmic fireball. It was only after that primordial fiery explosion had cooled down that energy, bound by the strong force of subatomic particles, or quarks, wove webs which created matter. Before the earth was formed, the atoms which made up its rocks and stones were adrift in space, some incorporated into ancient stars. The energy which makes your life possible comes from the hydrogen in our sun, which like everything else in the universe originated from that same primordial fireball. The molecules that make up your body were created from the death of stars billions upon billions of years ago. The universal law of gravity keeps your feet on the ground, and every rock and stone beneath your feet shares your origin from the beginning of time.

Quantum physics teaches that everyone and everything is interconnected through one giant web of life in which each of us is a part. Yet as I look at a tree I ask myself, how am I and the tree one? This may be a puzzle if my mental image is of a solid tree, but from the quantum perspective both the tree and I are essentially vibrating energy. I gain a sense of oneness with the tree by realizing that the only difference between us is that the atoms which make up my body and the atoms which make up the tree are vibrating at different frequencies.

The new science of ecology also shows how all aspects and creatures of our earth are interconnected, both locally and globally. For example, the great American conservationist John Muir wrote, "Whenever I try to pick out anything by itself, I find it hitched to everything else in the universe....[One example is a marsh.] We can start with one of the simplest life forms, the green algae. This slimy–looking stuff floats around in the water or grows on the stems and roots of other plants. Small animals such as the isopod eat the algae and are in turn eaten by predatory animals such as the dragonfly nymph. When the nymph crawls up on the stem of a marsh plant to shed its skin and become an adult, it becomes prey for Redwing Blackbirds. These birds are, in turn, prey for hawks."[41]

Finally, in contrast to Newtonian causality, which said that things happen because of chains of linear causality—event A causes event B which causes event C—the New Science teaches us that every event has multiple causes, and produces multiple effects. The more complex the system in which events take place, the more impacts an event will have. Since each of us participates not only as individuals in human society, but also as residents of this planet and as inhabitants of the larger universe, what we do can have impacts at every one of these levels, which demonstrates yet again how interconnected we all are.

Scientists express the interconnectedness of the universe by describing it as a seamless whole. Brian Swimme writes in *The Universe Is a Green Dragon,* "The universe is a coherent whole, a seamless multi–leveled creative event."[42] Menas Kafatos and Robert Nadeau write in *The Conscious Universe: Part and Whole in*

Modern Physical Theory that "The cosmos is a dynamic sea of energy manifesting itself in entangled quanta which results in a seamless wholeness on the most primary level, in seamlessly interconnected events on any level."[43]

The Universe Is a Whole

Newtonian science was based on the assumption of "reductionism," which focuses on isolated parts in order to explain all phenomena. The ultimate goal of reductionism is to reduce everything to its smallest parts in order to find the basic "building blocks" of the universe—which, it is assumed, group together in various configurations to form the wide variety of physical objects and living entities which populate the universe.

The basic assumption of reductionism is that by understanding the working of each part, you can understand the whole. But as Fritjof Capra writes in *The Tao of Physics,* "Quantum theory...reveals a basic oneness of the universe, it shows that we cannot decompose the world into independently existing smallest units. As we penetrate into matter, nature does not show us any isolated 'basic building blocks,' but rather appears as a complicated web of relations between the various parts of the whole."[44]

Instead of only breaking down phenomena into their smallest parts, scientists now study the *relationships* between the parts in order to understand how they interact to create the qualities and properties of the larger systems, or wholes, of which they are part. In the New Science, the study of reality in terms of wholes, called "holonomy," complements the reductionist approach. Holonomy reflects the concept of "holism," that an organism or integrated whole has a reality independent of and greater than the sum of its parts. The New Science has discovered that the only way to understand the properties of the parts is through the dynamics of the whole or as Fritjof Capra writes, "the universe...has to be pictured as one indivisible, dynamic whole whose parts are essentially interrelated and can be understood only as patterns of a cosmic process."[45]

Instead of talking about "hierarchy," holonomy talks about "holarchies," that is, continua among related wholes, based not on power and control but on increasing degrees of complexity. Each level of a holarchy is "nested" inside the next, larger and more complex level. For example, each of us is made up of atoms, which make up elements, which make up molecules, which make up cells, which make up tissues, which make up organs, which make up organ systems, which make up individual human beings, who are parts of human and ecological communities, which make up the earth, which is part of the solar system, which is part of the Milky Way galaxy, which is part of the Local Cluster of galaxies, which is part of the universe. Each of these entities or levels is whole in itself, but each also joins with others of its type to create larger wholes.

The philosopher Arthur Koestler called each smaller whole in a holarchy a "holon." A holon faces two ways: both up toward the larger whole of which it is part, and down toward its own smaller parts. For example, each cell in your body is a holon because it is both an individual entity, made up of its own molecules, atoms, etc. and it is also part of a larger tissue or organ. While the properties of the smaller wholes in a holarchy influence the characteristics of the larger whole that they constitute, the larger wholes have their own properties, which can influence their smaller components. It is reasonable to assume that this two–way orientation describes all holarchies, from the smallest, simplest organisms to the universe itself.

The Universe Is Intelligent

Scientists today observe a stunning variety of forms and phenomena throughout the universe, ranging from the simplest to the extremely complex, each continuing to change and evolve. Where reductionism said that the behavior of any entity could be predicted from what we know about its smallest components, the New Science asserts that the behaviors of more complex systems cannot be deduced from the laws which govern their more elementary parts. For example, while the atoms and molecules in a living system obey the physical laws which apply to all atoms and molecules, the activities of the larger living beings themselves follow their own distinct patterns and display their own distinct characteristics which may be markedly different from those predicted by the mechanistic laws of Newtonian physics. [46]

Therefore, many scientists now say that as the universe changes and evolves, it creates higher levels of complexity and self-organization, including intelligent and conscious beings, which operate according to their own more complex laws of behavior. Furthermore, the patterns which reproduce these complex forms are not simple physical patterns, but patterns of information, such as in our DNA. While these patterns of information may dictate some characteristics of their offspring, they establish only potentials and possibilities for other characteristics and behaviors, leaving their actualization up to many future factors, including the creativity and choices of the new organism. This is a very different view of the universe from the rigidly predictable Newtonian clockwork.

This new, infinitely more complex view of the universe has encouraged many scientists, theologians, philosophers, and other observers to propose that because the universe has the ability to create this vast complexity of numerous diverse patterns and entities, which includes living, intelligent, conscious beings; and because the universe uses information to do so, we can therefore describe the universe itself as having intelligence. That is, intelligence is not merely a local phenomenon arising from human brains, but in fact, intelligence is the ability of the universe to create these numerous, diverse, and continually evolving patterns and levels of organization. From this perspective, one could also say—as some scientists and theologians are now proposing—that "mind" has always pervaded the universe; that is, mind has always co–existed with matter, or perhaps more accurately, mind has always been inherent within matter.

In addition to many of the books already mentioned, other books by scientists which explore the intelligence of the universe include *The Elemental Mind* by Nick Herbert, *The Conscious Universe* by Menas Kafatos and Robert Nadeau, and *The Intelligent Universe* by Fred Hoyle. In *God and the New Physics,* the physicist Paul Davies writes:

There is a growing appreciation among scientists that neither mind, nor life, need to be limited to organic matter.....Now consciousness and intelligence are software concepts; it is only the pattern that counts, not the medium for its expression. Taken to its logical conclusion, it is possible to imagine a supermind existing since the creation, encompassing all the fundamental fields of nature, and taking upon itself the task of converting an incoherent big bang into the complex and orderly cosmos we now observe; all accomplished entirely within the framework of the laws of physics. This would not be a God who created everything by supernatural means, but a directing, controlling, universal mind pervading the cosmos and operating the laws of nature to achieve some specific purpose. We could describe this state of affairs by saying...that the universe is a mind: a self–observing as well as self–organizing system. Our own minds could then be viewed as localized 'islands' of consciousness in a sea of mind.... [47]

Erich Jantsch writes at the end of *The Self-Organizing Universe* that "God is the mind of the universe. By mind I mean the self-organizing principle of cohesion and organization that evolves as the universe evolves. Previously to now mystics have believed this but as scientists do it will move more fully into our culture." [48] The quantum physicist David Bohm writes, "The true state of affairs of the material world is wholeness. If we are fragmented, we must blame it on ourselves. In these terms we can 'infer' that human consciousness 'partakes of' or 'participates in' the conscious universe, and that the construct of the alienated mind, no matter how real feelings of alienation might be in psychological terms, is not in accord with scientific facts."[49] In answer to the question of how many minds he thought existed in the universe, the quantum physicist Erwin Shroedinger said, "If the sum total of the number of minds could be counted, there would be just one."[50]

Thus, the New Science is leading to the conclusion that your mind is a smaller aspect of the cosmic mind, and your life reflects the entire cosmos, in the same way that smaller levels of a holarchy are influenced by and reflect the larger levels of the holarchic continuum.

A Mystical View of Reality

The latest scientific discoveries are increasingly coming to resemble the core wisdom teachings of the world's great spiritual traditions: that the universe is intelligent, purposeful, and filled with mind (spirit); that everything is connected; and that each individual reflects and participates in the creative power of the cosmos.

For example, the discovery in modern physics that reality is created from a network of interconnected, mutual relations in which all things and events interact with each other is the same picture of reality presented by Eastern spiritual traditions. The term *Tantra,* as in Tantric Buddhism, is derived from a Sanskrit word meaning "to weave." For centuries, Tibetan Buddhism has taught the interwoven nature and interdependence of all events and things. Buddhism believes that the external world does not exist separately, but our outer and inner worlds are two faces of the same fabric, whose threads encompass all forces and events, and that both consciousness and all material objects are interwoven into an inseparable net of relations. In the Hindu religion, the god Brahma is believed to be the unifying thread in the cosmic web, the ultimate ground of being. Hinduism describes the whole which makes up the entire web of creation as the Soul.

The idea that the cosmic mind is in each of us is reflected in both Eastern and Western spirituality. In Christianity, Meister Eckhart called the cosmic mind the "Godseed." In Jewish mysticism it is referred to as "shekinah," the indwelling female presence of God. In Hinduism the cosmic presence within you is called *Atman*, which becomes one with the larger mind, the *Brahman,* and the realization that you and God are one is called the Brahman Splendor.

The New Science is also reflected in the spiritual philosophy of panentheism, which describes the inherent connection between the whole of creation and all of its individual parts. In this respect panentheism is a form of mystical spirituality. (Panentheism should not be confused with pantheism, which equates God with the external universe, and denies the existence of a personal God.) Matthew Fox writes:

Panentheism means "all things in God and God in all things." This is the way mystics envision the relationship of world, self, and God. Mechtild of Magdeburg, for example, says, "The day of my spiritual awakening was the day I saw and knew I saw all things in God and God in all things." Panentheism melts the dualism of inside and outside—like fish in water and the water in the fish, creation is in God and God is in creation.[51]

We are all part of a "cosmic continuum." We are all made of the same "universe-stuff." We are all interconnected through our interactions and relationships, and impact each other. We are all part of the holarchic ladder of nested wholes, ranging from the most minuscule sub–atomic particles to the largest forces of the universe. My physical body and energy partake of the matter and energy of the universe, and my mind reflects the cosmic intelligence, or mind of the universe.

I have felt great awe and meaning by realizing that I, too, am part of something as small as a quantum wave and as large as the universe; that each of us is a smaller cell in the body of life, shaped by the cosmic laws of the largest whole; and that each of us expresses the divine creative force of the universe. The insight that I am part of the creative process of the universe and an active participant in its evolution reinforces my sense of self–worth. This does not mean that I am God. We are all distinct individuals with our unique gifts, histories, and limitations. We each have a Shadow with which we must always deal. I am not perfect, nor do I ever expect to be so. You and I are always in process. While it is my responsibility to become aware of my sacredness as a part of this sacred universe, and to do my best to fulfill my personal mission in life, I must also remember that I am not alone. Not only is each of us sacred, but the universe is shaped by a larger design and intelligence, and I can connect to this larger intelligence, ask for help, and receive guidance from it.

The Principle of Universal Connectedness

Inspired by the discovery that the New Science can be reconciled with a spiritual perspective, and in particular, that the recent discoveries in physics, cosmology and other sciences support a mystic's conception of reality, I developed the sixth principle of the Balanced Paradigm: **The Principle of Universal Connectedness.**

> The universe is an intelligent, interconnected reality.
> **The Principle of Universal Connectedness**

I realized that an information-rich circular image, such as web pages (white dots) scattered over the Internet, can help us visualize how we participate in the Principle of Universal Connectedness. (See Figure 8.1.) Imagine that you are any point on this image. You are connected both inward and outward, and to any other point around the circle, just as they are all connected to you.

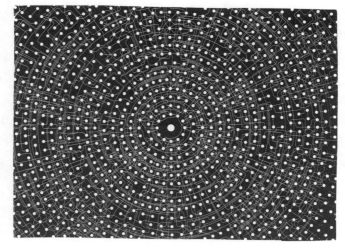

Figure 8.1.

Since there are larger patterns of design and intelligence in the universe, and since smaller wholes reflect and are influenced by the larger wholes to which they are connected through the cosmic continuum, this means that there is a larger universal intelligence or design which affects my life, and to which I can open up. I access the wisdom of the universe through its messages, which come to me beyond conscious awareness—through intuition, hunches, etc. And I invite the larger intelligence of the universe to guide my life, by releasing my need to control my world and allowing "meaningful coincidences" or "miracles" to happen to me. I believe that these are not unusual or supernatural occurrences, but that we can all experience them by opening up to the larger wisdom of the universe, if we so choose.

Opening up to Our Cosmic Connections

B.T., I had a powerful need to control my life and environment, and never wanted to be surprised. A.T., I began to understand that there is a higher consciousness or intelligence which guides our lives, and I could open up and connect to it. The Balanced Paradigm reminds me that I will never be completely rid of my Shadow or my fears, but whenever I center myself or remember that I don't have to control the process, I receive guidance or direction from a higher level. I believe this is not unique to me; any one of us can access this higher level of guidance as long as you are committed to doing the necessary personal work.

I experience this sense of higher direction in several ways. Whenever I turn my attention inward and ask for guidance, I receive it. I also use centering regularly to break through old fears, and limiting beliefs and open myself up to the larger universe. Guidance also comes to me regularly through hunches, intuition, and dreams. I believe that dreams, hunches, and intuition are a divine language which brings us messages from deep inside about our lives' purposes, and I pay attention to their messages and act on them.

Many successful and creative people acknowledge the importance of intuition in their lives. I have heard many businesspeople say that after getting all the relevant facts, they made the right decision by "listening to their gut." The Nobel-Prize-winning geneticist James Watson had been working for a long time trying to learn how the molecules in DNA fit together. After taking a break, Watson described what happened: "Suddenly I became aware...that both pairs could be flip–flopped over and still have their... bonds facing in the same direction. It strongly suggested that the backbones of the two chains run in opposite directions." This insight through intuition led to our understanding of how the patterns by which the characteristics of living beings are passed on. Another form of intuition tells us what to do without telling us why. This form of intuition often keeps us out of harm's way. For example, one evening in the fall of 1941, when London was under siege, Winston Churchill, who was known to be an active listener to his intuition, went out at night to visit antiaircraft batteries. As Churchill was leaving, his aide opened the customary door, but Churchill walked around the car and let himself in the far door instead. Immediately after he entered the car, a bomb exploded on its other side. If he had sat where he usually did, he would have been killed. When he got home his wife asked him why this time he sat on the other side of the car. He told her that "Something said to me, 'Stop!' before I reached the car door held open for me. It then appeared to me that I was told I was meant to open the door on the other side and get in and sit there—and that's what I did."

Another example of the warning aspect of intuition is the not-infrequent experience of a person about to board a plane and something inside tells him not to go. When such people trust their intuition, they change their travel plans, taking a later plane. It often turns out that the plane which they did not take crashed, killing all the people who were on it. The people who switched from the downed plane were guided by an unconscious sense that "this was not their time to leave this planet."

I personally experienced this warning intuition several years ago, when I was bringing my sailboat to a harbor south of Boston for winter storage. As I left Boston Harbor, I entered the open ocean where the waves were very rough. On this journey I would have to go past a rocky ledge that juts out underwater for over a mile and has been the graveyard for many ships over the centuries. As I approached this ledge, something deep inside me told me not to go on. I had never turned around in the middle of a sea journey before, but this internal message was so clear and definite, I then tried to come up with logical reasons why I should; my anchor would be useless since the water was too deep, and there were no other boats in sight to help me in case I got into trouble. I listened to my "gut" and went to a nearby marina. The next day I made a safe journey in calm seas. To this day I know that had I continued and not listened to my intuition, I might not be around today.

Opening up to Miracles

As I began to shift from feeling isolated and needing to be in control, and moved to feeling connected to the universe and all its inhabitants, meaningful coincidences, or "miracles," increasingly happened to me, bringing my life ever greater richness. Such strange coincidences happen to us all the time. For example, you might be thinking about someone and the next thing you know you bump into her on the street or get a phone call from him. Or you might unexpectedly meet people who turn out to be extremely significant in your life, be given help when you least expect it, or narrowly escape serious danger. We can discount such experiences as mere "coincidences," but I have come to believe that they are actually expressions of our cosmic interconnectedness, as the larger universe brings us its wisdom and guidance. I believe that by giving up control and trusting the process, we connect to the intelligence of the universe. Another way to say it is that we can learn how to allow miracles to happen to us.

I could share many stories about the "miracles" which have happened in my life. Here is a very dramatic example. One year I went to the boat yard to take my sailboat out of winter storage so I could move it to its summer docking in Boston Harbor. My father and I launched the boat and raised the mast, but I did not have time to secure everything since the weather was changing fast and this was the only time in my schedule when I could bring the boat on the 25 mile journey to Boston. I used the motor to get the sailboat to Boston, while my father, who gets seasick just by looking at a filled bathtub, drove down to meet me. After a three-hour sea journey with no problems, my boat's engine died right in the shipping channel to Boston Harbor. I thought, "Oh boy, am I in trouble!"

I could not use the sail since only one side of the mast was secured. I was able to keep the wind on the side where the mast was secured and in that way sailed up to the marina, but without an engine, how was I going to get into a slip? I noticed that an outside slip was open and tried to maneuver the boat into it. As I dropped the sails and approached the dock, I yelled, and my father and the marina manager ran down to help. I steered the boat as close as I could to the slip and jumped onto the dock, my left hand holding a line that was attached to the back of the boat. Once ashore, I quickly wrapped the line around the dock cleat in order to stop the boat, and prayed that the line would not break, since if my boat broke loose and kept on going, it would smash into several boats in the slips further ahead.

As the line pulled the six tons of boat to a screeching halt, I heard a cracking noise. My left hand was caught between the metal cleat and the line I was holding, and my fingers were squashed by the pressure. The marina manager yelled to two Boston policemen who kept their police boat at the marina. They put me into their police car and rushed me to the hospital while my father, my wife Judy, and Ken Hansen, an employee of my company who had come to meet me at the marina, all drove along behind. While sitting in the back seat of the police car I remember thinking, "This is not happening to me. I have no time for this."

All of a sudden we were at the Massachusetts General Hospital emergency room. The emergency team pulled off my wedding ring and X-rayed my hand. While the orthopedic surgeons were discussing my X–rays, my father, Judy and Ken arrived. The surgeons came over and informed us that they were astounded because my fingers were not broken. They returned my wedding ring (which I could not get back on since it was totally crushed). Ken Hansen, who had been an orthopedic technician in the operating room at Children's Hospital for ten years, simply looked at me and exclaimed "No way!" But the fact was that my fingers were not broken. We still talk about this incident in family discussions, and my father always shakes his head incredulously; he was there and saw it all.

I have experienced a sense of the miraculous at least four times in relation to the anniversary of Judy's death, which was of course an extremely significant event for me. As the first anniversary of her death approached, I wanted to do something special in remembrance of her. Since Judy had been a flight attendant, I felt it was appropriate to fly somewhere, so I decided to fly to Los Angeles with Justin, who was then three, to meet some friends and tour Southern California with them. We had a long delay before take–off because the mechanics were doing an extended inspection on our plane, since a few days before the same kind of plane had crashed due to mechanical problems. As we began flying, I remember thinking that at 11:00 P.M., the hour of Judy's death, I really did not want to be standing in line at a baggage counter or stuck in a men's room. But at exactly the hour she had died, Justin and I were 30,000 feet in the air and beginning our descent into Los Angeles, as a brilliant sunset over the Pacific Ocean illuminated the curvature of the earth.

On the second anniversary of Judy's death I was visiting Mohegan Island, off the coast of Maine, with a woman I was dating.

During the day, as I sat on rocks by myself, thinking and writing for this book, I noticed a seal's head emerge from the ocean approximately 200 feet in front of me. For more than two hours that seal and I were face to face. Later that evening, at exactly the hour of Judy's death, my woman friend and I were sitting on a dock when all of a sudden we both heard mysterious music coming from across the small harbor. We walked over and found a shell–covered beach. As small waves broke on the beach, the shells sang.

On the third anniversary of Judy's death, I was sitting on a dock in Nantucket Harbor. At exactly 11:00 p.m. I saw a vision of three people on a boat: myself, Justin, and another woman (not the woman I had been dating for three years). On the fourth anniversary I was at an inn on Cape Cod with Maureen, whom I had just begun to date. We were sitting on the balcony of our room, overlooking the ocean, and waiting for 11:00 p.m. The moonless night sky was black as velvet. At 11:00 p.m. a half moon suddenly appeared from behind the inn, lighting up first the ocean, then a sandbar, the beach, a tidal pool, then the other side of the beach. It felt especially significant for me that it was a half moon, since that conveyed a fundamental concept I was writing about at the time, that although we can only see the lighted half of the moon, there is a balancing dark half which makes the moon whole. I also felt that the dark side of this moon symbolized that Judy was gone, but she was still connected with me—the living, bright side—because I was now trying to get our message out. Also, at exactly 11:00 p.m. both Maureen and I heard a church bell chime eleven times. It was the only time that bell had chimed the whole evening. Maureen is quite attuned to hearing church bells because she lives next to two large churches, one whose bell rings every half hour, and the other whose bell rings every quarter hour. Both Maureen and I were astonished that we heard these bells only at 11:00 p.m. After Maureen and I married, no more such events happened, as if to say that I no longer needed such direct connection with Judy's spirit.

My connection with Maureen also developed through a series of "coincidences" and inexplicable events. After Judy's death, I started giving lectures about the Balanced Paradigm. At a Christmas gathering in a library where I had recently given a series of lectures, I got into a conversation with an unfamiliar man who came up to me. At the end of the discussion he said, "A Queen of Hearts is watching over you. She will make sure that the right person will fill her role as your son's mother." Since I had never met this man before and he knew nothing about me or my life's circumstances, I just stared at him. I did not know what to say except "Thanks" and "Happy Holidays."

Some time after this incident, a woman friend of mine called and described an acquaintance of hers, Maureen, whom she wanted me to meet because she thought we would be a good match. My friend had already described me to Maureen, who said it would be all right for me to call her. I was not really interested in meeting Maureen just then, since I was in the process of trying to develop a relationship with someone else, but out of respect for my friend, I called Maureen anyway. We agreed to meet for dinner at a restaurant outside of Boston, one which I had never been to, but which was convenient for Maureen since that evening she was returning from a work–related meeting in that vicinity.

Driving to the restaurant that night was extremely treacherous since it had been sleeting most of the day, but I arrived safely. I entered the restaurant, told the hostess that I was meeting someone there, and looked around, but saw only couples sitting at the tables, so I decided to go back out and wait for Maureen in the foyer. I waited 20, 35, 40 minutes. After an hour, I went outside, returned to my car and waited a little longer, watching for a single woman going into the restaurant. Since no one came and by now it had started to sleet again, I finally drove home.

While I was paying Justin's baby sitter, the phone rang. It was Maureen, who was concerned because I was not at the restaurant. She wondered if I had gotten lost or if something had happened to me while I was driving. I told her that I had waited at the restaurant for over an hour. She replied that the whole time I had been looking inside the restaurant, then waiting in the foyer, she had been sitting on a bench right inside the restaurant entrance where I first went in. Somehow I did not see her and she did not see me. I apologized, saying that in all my years nothing like this had ever happened to me. Several days later I called Maureen and left her a message, repeating that I was sorry about what had happened and that if she would like to try meeting again to please give me a call. I never heard from her.

A few months later the phone rang. It was Maureen. She told me that it was not her style to be rude, and she had felt bad about not responding to the message I had left. We agreed to try another restaurant, this time one we both knew. When we finally met we discovered that if we had met that first time, nothing would have come of it then, because both Maureen and I were in other relationships, which had since broken up. That night I met Maureen, who is now my wife.

Maureen is another miracle of the universe, flooding my life with love. As Meister Eckhart wrote in *The Soul Is One with God,*

"God is love, and he who lives in love is in God and God in him."
I have never met anyone with such unconditional love as my wife
Maureen. Kindness and loving acceptance are her very nature. The
people she works with as a special educator, and even strangers in
the supermarket and on the street are attracted to the magnetism of
her unconditional love.

Not only is Maureen my wife, but equally important, she is also
mother to Justin. Getting remarried was not just about me, but also
about how my son was going to be treated by a stepmother. We've
all heard horror stories about people marrying someone with a child
from a previous marriage, and the relationship turning into a
disaster. After losing his mother, the last thing Justin needed was a
bad stepmother or another loss through divorce. Maureen is an
incredible mother to Justin and has created an enveloping
atmosphere of love and encouragement in our home. She often
prays to Judy for guidance that she is doing the right thing for
Justin. Before we met, Maureen had never been married because
she would never compromise; she was waiting for the right person.
I'm so blessed she decided the right person was me.

The 20–year process of writing this book has also been filled
with "coincidences" and "miracles." For example, while at the
Harvard Divinity School I attended a lecture by Professor Harvey
Cox, the author of many successful books including the classic *The
Secular City*. During his talk, Dr. Cox quoted some material that I
wanted to refer to in my own book. After the symposium I went to
his office and was greeted by his secretary, who asked me about
what I was doing. I told her that I was in the process of writing a
book. She immediately offered to help me. On their own time,
Professor Cox's two secretaries typed the original manuscript of

this book, which allowed me to send it to a literary agent in New York City. This helped give Judy the peace of mind to die, knowing that this book was going to be a reality.

One thing that kept me going through all these years of working on this book was that the right book or the right article would always jump out at me. I have often felt as if I were standing on the last rock in a fast–moving stream, unable to take another step to cross the water, when suddenly another rock—that is, just the book I needed—would simply appear. It is an incredibly validating experience to know that the right book or whatever one needs will come into your life at just the right time!

One of many instances was while I was writing this chapter. Justin and I went to a bookstore in Harvard Square to look for a book on Egypt that he needed for his sixth grade class. While he was searching through the children's history section, I discovered a discounted section I had never seen before, and there found a book on the history of organizational development which I thought could be useful for the business book I plan to write next. I didn't buy it then, but a few weeks later, when Justin and I were back at the bookstore looking for a Mother's Day gift, I told him that I wanted to take a moment to look for the organizational book again. This time I couldn't find it, but a hardcover book on cosmology, for only four dollars, jumped out at me. I went over to Justin, knelt down and described to him what had just happened—how another "right" book yelled to me "Here I am!" I told him that when you trust the process, everything in your life works the way it should. That book, which I bought that day, gave me an enormous amount of new knowledge, and helped expand many of the concepts I had been working on.

Believing that miracles and guidance will come to me has helped me connect with my life's deeper purpose, which is in the process of emerging as I live, and has helped me trust the universe wholeheartedly from the deepest part of my being. Over and over, my life has confirmed the phrases "Ask, and you shall receive" and "When the student is ready, the teacher will come." What you receive might not be what you expected, but it will be exactly what you need for your personal growth.

Chapter 9

Living Our Interconnectedness:
The Principle of Love–in–Action

Discovering the Principle of Love–in–Action

While each of us is a unique being, with his or her own unique gifts and purpose for being, at another level we are all one, connected to every other living being through the sacred web of life. We can express our interconnectedness actively. If everything is interconnected, this means that everything which you or I do has an impact—far beyond ourselves. This perspective helps us understand that everything you and I do truly makes a difference.

All of the world's great spiritual traditions teach us that we are here on this earth to practice love and compassion toward our fellow beings. This means that you and I and every one of us can actively express our interconnectedness and the sacredness of all creation by choosing to act with love in everything we do. This sense of oneness also helps us become aware that our species is only one of many on earth, and that every time we make a species extinct, we are destroying a fellow manifestation of creation.

According to people who are in the process of dying, the only account which matters is not your bank account, but the amount of love which surrounds you. As Judy wrote in her farewell note to our two–and–a–half–year–old son, "I hardly know what to say to see you through the future. I wish I knew magic words to always make your road smooth, but that would not be living, because in order to compassion for one's fellow beings seem to be the place to start or the place to return to if you get stuck."

My journey of self–transformation has shown me that you can express love in every level of relationship: starting with love for yourself; moving out to those closest to you, your family and friends; moving further out to your interconnectedness with and love for people in your community, nation, and globally; and finally, expressing your interconnectedness with and love for all creatures on Earth, and love for our planet itself. Since all beings are interconnected, every act of love which you or I share will reverberate far beyond the immediate recipients, spreading both openly and unrecognized through the world, helping restore wholeness and healing the sacred web of life.

Reflecting on these insights inspired me to develop the seventh principle of the Balanced Paradigm: **The Principle of Love–in–Action.**

> We are all interconnected, and our purpose here is to express love and compassion for all beings (starting with yourself).
> **The Principle of Love–in–Action**

Many years ago I was attracted to a black and white mandala and, because it depicted balance, I decided to use it as a corporate logo for my new company, Innervisions. (See Figure 9.1.) Over the following years as I developed the seven principles of the Balanced Paradigm, I was amazed to realize that this mandala actually represents all seven principles. The Principle of Mutuality is reflected in the complementary black and white diamonds. The tips of each diamond connect with the diamonds next to it, thus creating a continuum. The inner circle represents your original core, your Center of Balance. The outside circle symbolizes both your wholeness and the wholeness of the universe and everything in it. When you look at this image it seems to vibrate, which represents both the universal process of dynamic balance, and your active expression of the Balanced Paradigm through Love–in–Action.

Figure 9.1.

Loving Oneself and Others

In order to become whole I had to learn to love myself first, to believe that—even with my faults and weaknesses—I was still worthy of love. B.T., I never really understood why other people loved me, since I did not love myself, and when you do not love yourself, it is hard to love anyone else or let anyone else truly love you.

As I became aware of and accepted all of myself, including my

Shadow, and gradually created positive alternatives to my negatives, I simultaneously became more whole and more able to love all of myself. Even though I make judgments about myself, describing some of my characteristics and behaviors as "negative" or "worth improving upon," I still accept and love myself. That is, I can be judgmental about my actions, but love myself wholeheartedly. This is another expression of dynamic balance.

I am able to love myself even more as I learn that I am a living part of an intelligent, interconnected universe, that I share the same divine spiritual energies which prevail throughout creation. I love myself because I can step outside the frantic race for material rewards and external success, and can connect with that quiet place within, which allows me to open up to the cosmic intelligence and interconnectedness of the universe. As these new conceptual understandings of the universe and my new experiences in self–transformation contributed to making me feel worthy of love, my natural, healthy feelings of self–love emerged, which then made it possible for me to form truly loving relationships with other people.

For many years I tried to find fulfillment, or wholeness, through relationships with women. After a while, I would realize that the other person was not meeting my needs and the relationship would fall apart. This happened over and over again. What I was looking for in the other person was impossible to find, since wholeness can only come from within. In actuality, I was always searching for the parts of myself which were missing.

As I became more whole and able to love myself, I began to value relationships with others, since I no longer believed that relationships were the exclusive domain of women. I enjoyed creating and reinforcing an atmosphere of love and of connection in all my relationships and would frequently tell friends that I loved them.

Love helped me move from an exclusive focus on meeting my own selfish needs, to feeling an unselfish concern for the needs of the other people in my life. Also, because I no longer base my relationships on a need for approval from other people, I was increasingly able to feel openness and a sincere desire to share with others what I was feeling. I now understand that every person has strengths and weaknesses, and my goal is to receive each person I meet with the same love and acceptance I give myself. At the same time I can set limits, so that I stay in touch with my own purpose and don't get pulled off track by other people's issues.

I am especially blessed to be able to share love and wholeness within my family circle, creating an atmosphere of encouragement and loving support. Maureen, Justin and I do this every day, in many ways. For example, every night our family says grace. Just before eating, we hold hands around the dinner table, creating a circle of love. Then Maureen, Justin, or I speak. Usually the person whose turn it is that day gives thanks for the privilege of another day of life and for the food that we are about to eat. We then expand the family circle to all our loved ones, to all the people we know who are facing a crisis in their lives, and to all the people around the world who are in need. We then ask blessings for difficult situations that various family members are facing. The other two members will invariably add a "P.S.", asking for a blessing for the person who has just said grace.

Our family also creates loving connection through spontaneous group hugs which allow us to share physical contact and affection. To keep communication channels open, we regularly have "sharing time," which we schedule outside our home, usually at a restaurant because this is neutral ground. During this time, each of us has the right to bring up any issue for discussion, either regarding his or her life overall or relating to some particular incident with another family member which needs clarification. Laughter and joking are also enriching and uplifting aspects of our family, which help to balance the natural frustrations and "downs" of daily living.

Since Maureen and I have decided to make each other the top priority in our lives, spending time together, just the two of us, is especially important. Every day we have "sharing time," a time for talking and being together, which balances the strong forces of divergence as we pursue our different careers. Since play balances the seriousness of life, we schedule a "play day" each month, or "play nights" several times a month. It does not matter where we go or how much or little we spend. The important thing is having the time to interact as a couple and to take an overview of our relationship by transcending the daily issues of married life. We make time for sharing physical affection, holding hands, hugging, etc. every day, which creates a general atmosphere of foreplay in our relationship. A spiritual perspective toward my marriage has allowed me to view the physical space of our bed as a sacred altar. It is there where we enact our ultimate expression of love. It is said that in some religious traditions, the angels look with envy on humans' ability to make physical love.

Maureen and I both feel very fortunate to be in such a loving relationship, which reinforces our desire to never take each other for granted. For my part, I know that the transformational changes I made and all the hard work I put into restoring my wholeness have made it possible for me to feel so happy and content in my marriage.

Since I am now capable of close, loving relationships, I am now also able to create true friendships. I especially value friendships with people who are able to be honest with me and help me become aware of when I am acting from my old issues and negative behavior. I value being able to do the same for them (although not everyone wants this). I believe that ideally, friends inspire each other to be courageous and unselfish, bringing out the best in each other by encouraging the other person to live up to their fullest potential.

As a further expression of my spiritual connection to other people, I consciously try to show respect to everyone with whom I interact, no matter who they are or what they do. I enjoy being thoughtful in daily life simply by holding a door or saying "Hello," "Please," or "Thank you," which automatically increases civility, something our society so desperately needs. I now express the oneness of the spirit among all of us by writing "Love," rather than "Regards" or "Sincerely" in notes and letters to friends or associates. I do this to convey the innate connection between my inner being and theirs, since the same spiritual center exists in all of us.

The Larger Community

An imbalanced focus on the external aspect of life is having serious negative consequences for our larger world. Our materialistic culture emphasizes *acquiring* more, not *loving* more. This is why the current model is inherently imbalanced and causing the negative effects we see and hear about every day.

I wholeheartedly acknowledge the positive benefits of the mechanistic model: its technological breakthroughs have allowed us to expand travel and communication, creating the basis for the further expansion of our consciousness to the cosmological and spiritual levels we are just beginning to move toward. We are also, however, suffering from the negative effects of the old paradigm. In the United States, imbalance is having a negative impact even on the middle class, since in recent years we have had a disproportionate redistribution of wealth upward, to the already wealthy. Our nation's increasing imbalance between our professional and personal lives is causing untold problems today in families and the larger society. Severe economic imbalances also exist at the global level, between First and Third World peoples, and between the nations of the northern and southern hemispheres. The affluent one–third of the world consumes most of the raw materials, including ores, metals, oil and other fossil fuels, at the expense of the rest of humanity. Two–thirds of the world's people don't have enough food, while the other third is trying to lose the weight they gained during the Christmas season.

The negative effects of global imbalances are also harming the natural environment, which affects everyone's health, no matter how rich or poor. We are in the process of destroying the protective skin of our planet by depleting the ozone layer which protects all life from the deadly ultraviolet rays of the sun. Imbalances are also destroying the very lungs of the planet by decimating forests throughout the world. By overemphasizing how much we can take *from* the earth, by depleting its natural resources with little attempt to give back, we are in the process of destroying both our lives and the lives of future generations.

The myth of progress is one of the most powerful forces in the world today because it promises us a golden age of prosperity, where science and technology will transform the earth into a material paradise with constantly rising incomes. This expectation of ever–increasing material prosperity has led to a one–sided emphasis on external progress at the expense of inner development. In our striving to create a material paradise, we have temporarily lost the inner meaning of progress.

Since we are all connected, the negative misuses of technology, wealth, and power harm us all. A more wholistic perspective can deepen our awareness so we are able to view technological advances as external manifestations of the creative evolutionary process now taking place in humanity's consciousness. This wholistic approach also gives us the wisdom to understand that with every major technological advance humanity must develop a complementary inner advance, to balance the potentially negative use of the new technology. This broader consciousness can remind us that breakthroughs in technology represent our connections to the larger cosmos, since new technologies are made possible by our expanded scientific awareness of how the universe works.

The Balanced Paradigm is not just a model for individual transformation, or for self–contemplation, but is also the foundation from which each of us can become a responsible, compassionate co–creator of our larger world. Our inner personal transformation must be balanced with loving interactions with other people—not only with those we know intimately, but with fellow members of the larger local, national, and global communities in which we reside.

Deepening our spirituality allows us to experience unconditional love, which attunes our lives to the loving interconnectedness of the cosmos. This sense of cosmic unconditional love is not for your exclusive use alone, but needs to be compassionately shared with all people, especially those who are suffering. Your life can become a vehicle through which divine love becomes manifested in our everyday world through individual acts of love and by helping to create social justice in our society.

The Balanced Paradigm is a model for social and civic responsibility, encouraging each of us to take personal responsibility for creating a more just, peaceful, and humane society for the 21st century. The personal transformational changes you make can have positive effects on larger economic and social problems, such as education, health care, homelessness, and other forms of economic and social deprivation. You become aware of social and economic problems in your community, accept their presence but not agree with them, and you act creatively to alleviate them.

A higher level of cosmic consciousness helps you understand that all the various manifestations of divine creation on this planet are included in a larger view of community. Expanding your sense of community, allows you to participate in humanity's evolutionary process by helping to co–create a fair and equitable society and a better world.

Love–in–Action Toward the Planet Earth

In the emerging consciousness of the 21st century, reverence for the divine creative force of the universe (commonly referred to as "God") can be expanded from an hour in church once a week to a daily reverence for all of creation, since we see the sacredness in all human and non–human beings and throughout nature. This perspective can help us understand federal laws to protect the environment not as an intrusion, but as a responsibility and a privilege to help protect creation; to see the protection of endangered species not as a burden, but as the ability to protect a unique manifestation of creation.

The negative fruits of the mechanistic paradigm have shown themselves clearly in the North American continent. In 350 years the forests of this once pristine land have become denuded, our water toxified, many of our lakes lifeless, our topsoil impoverished, and our air poisoned, all in the name of "progress." According to the World Resources Institute, in the past 200 years the United States has lost 50 percent of its wetlands, 90 percent of its northwestern old–growth forests, 99 percent of its tall grass prairie, up to 490 species of native plants and animals have become extinct, and 9,000 species are now at risk.[52]

As I view myself and the world from a wholisitic perspective, understanding our universal connectedness, I become aware that my body is 90 percent water. Thus, I am connected to all the water on this planet. Yet we continue to pollute our rivers, lakes, oceans, and even the underground aquifers from which we get our drinking water. It takes an aquifer thousands of years to clean itself. It takes 100,000 years to deposit a few inches of fertile soil, yet each year we are washing away six million tons of topsoil in this country alone. Every day 40,000 children in this world die of hunger; we are destroying over one million species every decade; ever year, 240 million tons of poison created in this country alone are finding their way back into our bodies and changing the chemicals essential for the life of our species, in our DNA.[53] Experts warn that the number of birth defects and the incidence of autistic children are rising steadily in this country, and that glaciers all around the world are melting because of global warming. Most of the consequences of these short–sighted actions will not occur in my lifetime, but I keep asking myself: Don't we have a responsibility to our children and their children, and for the very survival of our species? I believe that we do.

Hearing such devastating statistics can be emotionally overwhelming and even paralyzing. It can make us give up in despair. This is where a balanced, spiritual perspective can give us power, hope, and guide our actions. Such a perspective can help us see that our prosperity need not be achieved at the expense of the earth's well–being. In our actions we can move beyond viewing the earth only as a resource to be exploited; we can give back to, as well as take from the earth.

When I was trapped in the insatiable cycle of materialism, I spent all my time and energy working to make money so I could buy possessions. After a brief sense of satisfaction I would then spend more time and money maintaining these material objects, or worrying about how they might be lost or stolen. Since I had no inner life, all that was important was the superficial, having the "right" possessions.

I became free from the incessant cycle created by commercial propaganda by realizing that the goal of all commercial advertisements is to make me unhappy with what I currently own. The essence of any advertisement is to create a need in our minds, and then show us how the products or services it sells can fill this so–called need. Many advertisements actually promise us that by using their products, we will experience our inner nature. For example, a billboard shows a Heineken beer label, with the statement "Seek the truth;" a Volvo radio ad says "Find your soul;" and *Barron's* newspaper claims it will help you "Find your inner Rockefeller."

Not only will the average American child be exposed to more than 30,000 commercials before he or she walks into first grade, but commercials are now being shown in many schoolrooms across the country. All of them preach the message that buying is what is of importance in life. To quote Brian Swimme,

> "Advertisements are where our children receive their cosmology, their basic grasp of the world's meaning, which amounts to their primary religious faith, though unrecognized as such. I use the word 'faith' here to mean cosmology on the personal level. Faith is that which a person holds to be hard-boiled truth about reality. The advertisement is our culture's primary vehicle for providing our children with their personal cosmologies....we live in a culture that has replaced authentic spiritual development with the advertisement's crass materialism."[54]

Both our spirits and the earth are being irreparably damaged by the "religion" of consumerism. Consumerism has its "priests"—the advertising agencies; its daily sermons are its messages, from television, radio, newspapers, magazines, mail, blimps, roadside billboards, on the sides of buses, even logos on the clothes that we wear. Shopping malls are the temples of the "religion" of consumerism, and its belief system is materialism. It's not a coincidence that Webster's Dictionary defines a "consumer" as "a person or thing that destroys, uses or wastes something."

I discovered that I could participate in the preservation of life on this planet by simplifying my own material life. I found it easier to do this when I became aware of the inherent negativity of a consumer–oriented lifestyle. Also, when I was trapped in the possession cycle, I never had time or energy for connecting with my true self. Truth, meaning, and my soul are not found in buying beer, cars, or other products but only in self-realization through an inner journey. Becoming free from an obsession with material possessions has made my life much easier. I am able to focus on what is really important, which has helped me transform both the way I buy and how I treat the earth in my daily life.

I no longer own a sailboat, and Maureen, Justin and I live in a comfortable five–room apartment. When I have a need to sail, we charter a sailboat. To simplify my life even further, I now consider two questions before I purchase anything. First, do I really need this, or am I buying it to feed my ego? Second, is there a "cost–in–use" alternative to what I am buying? This approach is based on the win-win fact that it is better to pay more initially for something which will last in the long run, because when its cost is averaged out over time, its use is less expensive. In general, it is more expensive to buy cheap things of poor quality, since you eventually have to go out and buy two or three replacements during the same period of time that you would have been using the higher quality product. I still own the car that I bought in Stuttgart 19 years ago. It looks almost brand new and in the past 16 years I have had no car payments, which has saved me at least $52,000.

The earth also wins through this cost–in–use approach to buying, since quality products have a longer life, which means that fewer materials were used up to make their replacements and therefore there is less trash for the earth to absorb. When you buy products of poor quality, or "garbage," it adds to the tons of garbage blanketing our earth.

A New Relationship Between Humanity and the Earth

A more wholistic, cosmic perspective allows us to become aware that our life is part of the earth's story, which is part of the story of the unfolding universe. This scientific cosmology can provide us with a unifying framework for restoring ecological balance to our endangered planet. We can discover intellectually and understand spiritually that our well–being is directly connected with the well–being of the earth, since if we continue to impair the life–supporting systems of the earth, we will be shutting down the very systems that keep us alive. Breaking out of the mechanistic world view, allows us to see the world in a different light. Realizing that the earth is sacred helps us to become active in creating ecological sustainability.

This new scientific perspective includes the spiritual perspective which many other cultures already have in relation to the natural environment. For instance, many North American native peoples saw both the sacred and the mundane in all of nature. The Lakota Sioux Chief Luther Standing Bear wrote that when man turns his

" heart from nature it becomes hard; he knew that lack of respect for living growing things soon led to lack of respect for humans too." A chief characteristic of the "old time religion" of the Celtic civilization, which existed throughout Western Europe before it was destroyed by the Roman legions and their religion, was connection with the wholeness of creation. In *Turning the Tide*, David Bellamy and Brendan Quayle note that in tribal societies

> there was no separation between culture and nature, between the lives of men and the natural world around them. And from them that interdependence was fused with the omniscience of the spiritual or creator world, the very power which they believed guided their existence in the world. [55]

In 1948, Fred Hoyle predicted that "once a photograph of the earth, taken from *the outside*, is available...a new idea as powerful as any in history will be let loose." His prediction came true in 1969 with the first pictures of earth floating in the blackness of space. As Jacques–Yves Cousteau wrote,

> the meaning of space conquest is symbolized by the famous set of pictures taken from the moon, celebrating the birth of a global consciousness that will help build a peaceful future for humankind. That future is in the hands of those who dedicate their lives to explore...[the] three infinites: the infinitely big, the infinitely small, and the infinitely complex. And from all the beauty they discover while crossing perpetually receding frontiers, they develop for nature and for humankind an infinite love.[56]

The first pictures of earth from space, taken by American astronaut John Glenn—and the pictures that are taken from space today—show conclusively that there has been an increase in pollution all around the world. The Russian cosmonaut Yuri Artyukhin stated, "It isn't important in which sea or lake you observe a slick of pollution, or in the forests of which country a fire breaks out, or on which continent a hurricane arises. You are standing guard over the whole of our earth."[57] German astronaut Ernest Messerschmid said that "when the Russian cosmonaut tells me that the atmosphere over Lake Baikal is as polluted as it is over Europe, and when the American astronaut tells me that fifteen years ago he could take much clearer pictures of the industrial centers than today, then I am getting concerned." [58]

This picture of earth from outer space is a unifying image in the emergence of our new consciousness. It allows us to become aware of the inherent unity of all life on this vulnerable planet. We can learn great insight and wisdom from the human beings who have been privileged to see the planet Earth from space. For example, John Glenn wrote, "in space one has the inescapable impression that there is a virgin area of the universe in which civilized man, for the first time, has the opportunity to learn and grow without the influence of ancient pressures. Like the mind of a child, it is yet untainted with acquired fears, hates, freed from prejudice."[59] USSR's Aleksi Leonov said that "the earth was small, light blue, and so touchingly alone; our home must be defended like a holy relic. The earth was absolutely round. I believe I never knew what the word round meant until I saw Earth from space."[60] James Irwin from the U. S. wrote that the Earth, "beautiful, warm, living object looked so fragile, so delicate, that if you touched it with a finger it would crumble and fall apart. Seeing this has to change a man, has to make a man appreciate the creation of God and the love of God."[61]

Astronaut Taylor Wang recalled "a Chinese tale [which] tells of some men sent to harm a young girl who, upon seeing her beauty, become her protectors rather than her violators. That's how I felt seeing the Earth for the first time. I could not help but love and cherish her."[62] Vladimir Kovalyonok realized after looking at Earth from space that "we are all sailing in the same boat."[63] Muhammad Ahmad Faris from Syria stated that "from space I saw Earth—indescribably beautiful with the scars of national boundaries gone."[64] Cosmonaut Pham Tuan from Vietnam said, "I realized that mankind needs height primarily to better know our long suffering Earth, to see what cannot be seen close up." [65] American astronaut John–David Bartoe wrote "two words leaped to mind as I looked down on all this: commonality and interdependence. We are one–world."[66] Alexander Aleksandrov from the USSR said that "it struck me that we are all children of our Earth. It does not matter what country you look at. We are all Earth's children, and we should treat her as our Mother."[67]

A Long–Term Vision for Humanity

I believe that as a species we are currently in the process of transformation to a new paradigm and to a higher level of consciousness. This has been made possible by many recent developments, including environmental awareness, the women's movement, exposure to non–Western philosophies, and through the most modern technological advances. Computers and satellite communications daily present us with pictures of Earth. International aviation, the World Wide Web, and the globalization of businesses are each creating a synthesis in the creation of a larger global consciousness. Major media events, such as pictures of the first time a man walked on the moon, or the funeral of Princess Diana, become part of the collective, global consciousness of our species.

The higher level of cosmic consciousness has allowed me, and can allow you, to become a visionary. Vision is defined by Webster's Dictionary as "the ability to perceive something not actually visible, as through mental acuteness or keen foresight, the force or power of the imagination...." The wholistic perspective created by the Balanced Paradigm has allowed me to see the "big picture" and deeper patterns of long–term trends. I do not know what is going to happen to me on a daily basis, but I do know the vision and mission of my life. Countless times I have told family and friends to watch a current event that was happening since it was part of a political, social or economic long–term trend.

I see two visions for the 21st century. In the first vision our species no longer exists, because we were afraid to change. We stayed addicted to outdated limiting beliefs, refused to transform our illusionary way of thinking, and valued security and comfort over integrity and truth. Because of our greed and refusal to change, we were unwilling to stop abusing the planet. Our addiction to fossil fuel destroyed the protective ozone layer of the earth, and the climate killed us.

The second vision is positive. In it, our species has evolved to its rightful inheritance because we opened our minds, which allowed us to become aware that human consciousness is a smaller part of the larger consciousness of the universe. We grew beyond an adolescent need to think that we have all the answers, and were completely independent, into the realization that our individual lives, and the human species in general, are small parts of the vast web of life and just one manifestation of the mystery of creation. A critical mass of people grew beyond the addictive need for the false security found in always being told what to believe and do. They appreciated and stood up for the opportunity to think for themselves and found their own inner paths to the Divine. New scientific discoveries about the universe, made possible by technologically sophisticated telescopes, expanded our concept of who we were, undermining our species' egotistical assumption that life exists only on this planet and that the universe revolves around us. We matured to the point where we could see that by polluting our environment, we were destroying our home.

Our species entered adulthood when large numbers of people broke free from the old paradigms and dysfunctional ways of living. They stopped living in fear and insecurity because they had the courage to take a heroic inner journey through their Shadows and to their souls. They married the inner, feminine aspect of their souls with the outer, masculine aspect of technology and business. They saw that a short–term focus and an imbalanced economic system, which always takes and never gives back, had self–destructed. This provided both the space and resources for a more balanced, sustainable, wholistic economic system to evolve.

The higher level of consciousness that emerged in the beginning years of the 21st century allowed a spiritual perspective to evolve in human consciousness. This enabled us to see our lives, other people, our work organizations, technology, the planet earth, and the universe from a sacred point of view. We became mature enough to model our lives on the principles of the universe and to connect with the wholeness and creative evolutionary process of the cosmos. We became responsible local citizens of the cosmos by realizing that we were inherently co–creators with the evolutionary process of the universe; that our lives were individual manifestations of "Being becoming" through the process of evolution. Because of the higher level of consciousness that we had attained, we became aware that we create the world each day by choosing our attitudes and beliefs, then acting on them. A cosmic perspective opened our lives to our original inner cores, which allowed the creativity of the universe to flow into our lives.

This second vision can become our reality. Because of the inherent interconnectedness of the universe, which is also within each of us, our individual awarenesses are connected which means that we can co–create the larger collective consciousness of our species. You can help create a new, harmonious world in which to live by taking responsibility for transforming your own consciousness. When enough people choose to develop and act from the balanced, wholistic paradigm, this will naturally have a positive influence on the consciousness of our planet. We can help co–evolve with the intelligent creative process of the universe. When a critical mass is reached, we will then create a positive alternative to the negative actions and beliefs of today's world.

Living your life in connection with the consciousness of the universe allows the following nine beatitudes to emerge. They are my parting gifts to you.

Beatitudes for the 21st Century

Blessed are you who search for truth;
  you will find it.

Blessed are you who are aware of your Shadow;
  you will become whole.

Blessed are you who experience the power of balance;
  yours is connection with your soul.

Blessed are you who live in the center of your being;
  yours is the divine kingdom.

Blessed are you who awaken;
  yours is cosmic consciousness.

Blessed are you who are spiritual;
  you will experience the spirituality that
  surrounds you.

Blessed are you who are loving and compassionate;
  you are a gift of the universe.

Blessed are you who realize that All is One;
  you are a blessing to the rest of the world.

Appendix A

Meeting Your Shadow
and
Building Positive Alternatives

This section provides questions which you can use in your own transformation process. You can work with them in three ways: on your own; in a dyad (two–person) format; and through a transformational group. I recommend using at least two, if not all of these methods.

Working alone has the advantage that you can do it at any time. However, because working with other people helps to eliminate the feeling of being isolated and provides objectivity and feedback, the dyad and group approaches are recommended to increase your learning, provide you with additional support, and further affirm your transformational process.

In a dyad model, two people meet on a weekly or biweekly basis in a structured format, with the goal of helping each other's personal and spiritual growth. The preferred meeting place should be a neutral setting, not at either person's home or workplace. Social pleasantries need to be limited to insure that sufficient time will be available for working. There are three rules for a dyad meeting:

1. What is discussed during the meeting is kept confidential between the two parties.

2. A specific time format needs to be agreed upon during the first meeting and closely adhered to in subsequent dyad meetings. For example, five minutes for pleasantries, 25 minutes for each partner to speak, and five minutes at the end for making future plans.

3. Discussions must be limited to the time of the dyad meeting. Under no circumstance should either member call the other between

meetings in order to make additional points. They need to be held until the next meeting. Each dyad meeting should end with establishing a time and place for the next meeting.

Each dyad meeting is divided into equal halves. During the first half, person "A" assumes the role of speaker while person "B" assumes the role of active listener. The speaker can discuss any issues he or she is currently dealing with, or something that was previously discussed, or additional insights that might have emerged from the last meeting. It is the responsibility of the active listener to ask gentle, loving, pertinent questions that encourage the speaker to keep talking. In order for the meeting not to become an intellectual exercise, the active listener needs to ask whenever appropriate: "How do you *feel* about that?"

After person A has finished, person B does three things: First, affirm the speaker for dealing with his issues. Second, share insights which arose while listening. Third, suggest something the speaker can work on between now and the next meeting, which will help further the growth process.

During the second half of the meeting, the same rules and format are used, but the roles are reversed. The active listener now becomes the speaker, while the first speaker is now the listener.

In order for the dyad process to be effective, it is recommended that partners meet weekly for at least four months. After that you can discuss if you want to keep going, and for how long. The intimate sharing that takes place in a transformational dyad often creates a deep bond of friendship that lasts over the years. I still see my dyad partner after sixteen years.

One's transformational process can be further enhanced by working in a group. A transformational group is made up of people who are dedicated to transforming their lives, and who choose to meet regularly for the expressed purpose of helping each other grow. Ten is the most efficient number for many group activities, including a transformational group; seven is recommended as a minimum and twelve as a maximum.

A transformational group demonstrates that the more you share with other people, the more you can learn about yourself. The group allows other people to really get to know who you are, and allows them to "call" you on your issues, which is a great way to become more aware of one's habits of denial and projection. Confidentiality also applies to a transformational group.

The group needs to agree upon a regular schedule of meeting times and places and all the members need to make a commitment to attend future meetings, which ensures that the dynamics of the transformational process will not be hindered by lack of participants. Also, making a personal commitment to the other members to attend meetings counteracts one's tendency to run away from working on individual barriers to personal growth.

During the first meeting the members together select a material object which will symbolize both the wisdom of each individual and of the group as a whole. This "wisdom object" should be fairly small and easy to hold, since whoever is speaking holds it.

In a transformational group, people sit in a circle. One person holds the wisdom object and speaks, while all the other members provide a silent, nurturing, supporting, loving environment. Only after the speaker has finished can anyone else in the group share insights, perhaps from similar experiences, or which emerged from listening to the speaker. Responses should be concise and focused on the issues of the person who has just spoken, not on one's own issues. The wisdom object is then passed to the next person in the circle, and that person becomes the speaker, while the others listen without interrupting, then respond.

Each transformational group meeting should end with some special group activity, such as a dance, song, or ritual that the group decides upon. This activity celebrates the people you are, the courage all of you are displaying in doing your personal growth work, and the potential within each and every one of you.

You can also choose a member of your transformational group to be your dyad partner, an especially effective way of furthering your healing process, since your sharing within the group allows your dyad partner to better know who you are.

Local transformational groups and dyad partners will be formed from the attendees of Innervisions' *Transforming your Life through the Power of Balance Seminars*.™ Call 1-800-677-6715, toll–free anywhere in the United States for information on when and where the seminars will be held in your area. You can also contact local holistic health programs or education centers to find other people interested in participating in personal growth work.

Exercises for Exploring Your Shadow

The following exercises begin with your inner feeling state and move on to how you perceive the world, act and react to events and situations in your life. These questions are designed to "dig deep." It might take you a day or more to think about just one question, since the answers have been stored away for a lifetime.

1. "Awareness Exercise"
The questions below can help you begin to release repressed negatives which may have been controlling you for years.
A. *What am I most afraid of in my life?*
B. *Whom have I hurt most in my life, and how?*
C. *What do I believe is the worst thing I have ever done?*
D. *What are the last things I'd want people to know about me?*

2. "Negativity in Your Life Exercise"
This exercise can help you become more aware of how your Shadow's negative conditioning has influenced your life. Take time to think about and answer the following questions:
A. *Do you have inferiority feelings? If so, what do you feel inferior about?*
B. *Do you feel unworthy, bad, defective? If so why?*

C. Do you feel that you were never really loved? If so, why?

3. "I Forgive Exercise"

After becoming aware of the contents of your Shadow, the next step is forgiveness, which allows you to create new connections in your life.

The first part of this exercise helps you begin to dissolve your Shadow by forgiving *yourself* for the wrongs you have committed towards others over the years, for example by being selfish or otherwise acting in hurtful ways. Forgiving yourself creates a psychological space in which a loving reinterpretation of your past can emerge. How would you complete this statement?

I forgive myself for:

In the second part of the "*I Forgive Exercise*" you forgive all the other people in your life, which helps free you from the effects of negative actions that others have done to you in the past. Complete the following statements as they pertain to your life.

I forgive my mother for:
I forgive my father for:
I forgive my sister for:
I forgive my brother for:
I forgive my relatives for:
I forgive my teacher(s) for:
I forgive my spouse for:
I forgive my "ex" for:
I forgive my "significant other" for:
I forgive my employer for:
I forgive anyone else for:

4. "Looking at Yourself Exercise."

Have you ever known people who don't like having their picture taken, and don't like to look at themselves? Their unconscious fear is that looking at themselves may trigger unwanted images and feelings stored in their Shadow. A simple yet effective technique for reconnecting with the long-held pain repressed in your Shadow is to *stare at your face—and especially into your eyes—in a mirror*. A good time to do this is before or after you brush your teeth in the morning or evening.

This simple technique can be very difficult to do. I used to close my eyes or walk around the house while brushing my teeth, anything to avoid looking at myself. The amount of resistance you encounter reflects the degree of your pain, but keep on really looking at yourself. You can do it! Since the "eyes are the mirror of the soul," you will eventually be able to see into the love that exists at your very core, underneath your Shadow.

5. "Shadow Talk Journal"

Assuming responsibility for your unrecognized negativity can provide a practical foundation for your process of change. Taking personal responsibility undermines two key aspects of one's Shadow: denial, which makes us unaware of the existence of our own negative aspect; and projection, that is, projecting our own negativity onto other people.

A "Shadow Talk Journal" brings your Shadow to light, eliminating its unconscious need to continually repeat the same old negative messages over and over. And you will find that the more you use this Journal to explore your Shadow and befriend your long–buried negative aspects, the less they undermine your conscious efforts to become more positive and whole.

This is how the Shadow Talk Journal works: Whenever you feel self-critical or hear yourself giving yourself a negative message (either in your mind or out loud), write the letters *WWFT* vertically down the left side of a notebook, leaving a few lines of space after each letter. Then next to each letter, write your answer to the question it represents.

The first *W* stands for *What*—"*What* negative message am I giving myself?" As you become aware of and acknowledge what your Shadow is saying to you, write it down, and also *say* this message out loud. This allows your "Shadow Talk" to have a conscious voice.

Next, try to associate each negative message with a person in your life who originally gave you that message. The second *W* stands for *Who*—"*Who* in my life does this message most sound like?" In this way, whenever you give yourself that same message later on, you will be able to say, "Oh! There goes So-and-So's negative message, trying to run my life again." This helps you separate who *you* really are from the other person's message.

The letter *F* stands for "*Feelings*," as in "How does this negative message make me *feel?*" Writing down the answer to this question helps you get more in touch with your feeling state. And the letter *T* stands for "*Trigger,*" that is, "What specific beliefs, circumstances, or feelings have *triggered* this message?"

Use this *WWFT* question-and-answer process each time you feel self-critical, or sense a negative message coming to you from inside. By bringing your Shadow to light through answering such questions, you become increasingly able to make a conscious decision either to continue to obey your Shadow's negative messages, or to choose alternative, positive messages. As you consciously become responsible for creating new messages to live by, this moves you further towards wholeness.

Here's an example of how this process worked for me. I felt that I had said the wrong thing to someone, and felt really bad about myself. So in my Shadow Talk Journal, after writing down *WWFT*, beside the first *W* I wrote down the negative message I was giving myself: "How dumb I was!" When I said this statement out loud, I could hear its critical, judgmental tone. Next to the second *W* I wrote down that this message actually sounded like my mother's voice. Next to *F* I wrote that the message made me feel like a failure. Next to *T* I wrote down that this message triggered my conditioned belief that I must never make a mistake. When I looked at what I had written down, I realized it was unreasonable to blame myself every time something went wrong, and I was then able to let this negative message go.

You might also want to explore the source of your negative messages in a trusting and supportive environment, for example, with the help of a counselor. If you have a specific issue or addiction, such as alcohol, drugs, food abuse, gambling, being a child or spouse of an alcoholic, etc., you can also join a support group to help you work on recovery.

Exercises for Creating Positive Alternatives

Since our mental pictures—what we feel and believe—energize our emotions and create each individual's personal reality, we need to balance our negative mental pictures with positive mental images of ourselves that evoke feelings of joy and love. The more you can "feel" as well as "see" the new positive image, the more your mental imagery is strengthened, so the key to this process is to create vivid and detailed pictures.

1. If you were made to feel inadequate by hearing that "you are not worth it," "you're no good" or "you'll never amount to anything," you probably pulled back and stopped trying. To create a counterbalancing image, picture yourself in detail as a person who is worthy of achieving what you really want in life.

Create a vivid picture of yourself achieving your goals.

2. For many of us it has been a long time since we knew what our own physical, spiritual, emotional or other needs were. Perhaps you were made to feel worthless or always taught to meet other people's needs at your own expense. You deserve to honor your own needs.

Create a vivid picture of what your physical, spiritual, emotional or other needs are.

3. Once you have discovered what your neglected needs are, you can then take responsibility for filling them.

Create a vivid picture of you meeting your own needs.

4. In our lifelong project of creating and maintaining a False Self, many of us never really became aware of our truly positive aspects. Answer the following questions:

What am I really good at?

What do I really enjoy doing?

If I could hear my eulogy, what positive contributions would I want to be remembered for?

5. Now you are ready to create a new, positively balanced self–image. You do this by describing yourself to yourself in a new way—a way that you want to be for the rest of your life.

Envision yourself as clearly and with as much detail as possible, being and acting in this new way.

Now ask yourself: *What practical things do I need to do to bring this new image of myself into reality?*

6. Many spiritual traditions teach that there is an infinite supply of goodness in the universe. You deserve to receive this goodness.

Picture yourself being open to receiving into your life right now the goodness, love, and harmony which exist throughout the universe and here on Earth.

7. One aspect of receiving goodness is to have fun.

Create a vivid picture of yourself having fun. What are you doing?

8. Since negative self–images are the saboteurs of financial success:

Create a vivid picture of yourself enjoying material success.

Appendix B

Centering Techniques

1. The Sound Centering Technique

To practice this technique, first choose a word or simple phrase that has meaning for you personally, or you can simply choose a nonsense syllable which feels calming. A word that has a special meaning for you, such as "God," "love," "one," "peace," "light," or a short phrase such as "God and I are one," "I AM," or "I am a son/daughter of God" will be especially helpful in allowing you to stay silent and relaxed in the center of your being. The right word will speak to you. It might stay with you for the rest of your life, or it may change in a twenty–minute period. You can also use a focusing sound or "mantra" such as "OM" (pronounced OHHH—MMM) to help center. By focusing your attention only on a sound, you focus your mind. The repetition of a sound or simple phrase detaches you from both internal and external distractions, because the rhythm reduces the electrical rate of your brain.

Sit quietly as described in Chapter 4 and breathe in and out slowly. As you continue to breathe in and out, repeat your sound either vocally or mentally, to coordinate with every inhale and every exhale. Continue to do this for 20 minutes. Listening to chant or meditative audio–cassettes also quiets your brain waves and helps center your mind by reducing your brain's electrical patterns to alpha.

2. The Awareness Centering Technique

Focusing your awareness enhances your ability to let go of the constant stream of inner chatter, worry and concern. It has been documented that most of us talk to ourselves 80 percent of the time and have approximately 16,000 thoughts per day. This constant inner conversation is usually loaded with emotional content such as guilt, resentment, hostility, or anxiety. We may replay good–time memories also, but guilt and resentment usually occupy the majority of our attention. This negative self–talk actually has consequences for our health, since our whole body responds to our mental images. As we think about and feel negative emotions, our muscles tighten, and we experience a stress response.

The Awareness Centering Technique helps you become detached from any particular thought. You step back and watch the constantly streaming train of thoughts flow through your mind as if you were watching a speeding freight train go by. You are able to see the blur of the rolling line of box cars, but do not focus your attention on any single car.

If, while you are centering, your mind becomes distracted by the contents of a thought, don't worry. Instead, simply return to your center by letting go of the idea. An analogy is lying in a grassy field watching fluffy clouds drift by on a beautiful summer day.

A quick way that I use the Awareness Centering Technique is by imagining a plastic tube filled with water, and an enclosed sphere of colored oil floating inside it. The colored oil is analogous to my inner awareness. When I become totally distracted by the issues of the day, they seem all encompassing and I am not in touch with my inner awareness. It is as if the water–filled tube is lying at a slight angle and the colored sphere has floated up out of the way to one corner of the tube. In order to reconnect with my inner awareness, I focus my attention on my breathing and imagine my awareness back inside me, as if the tube is standing upright which allows the oil to float directly to the top of the tube, where it is now centered in the middle of my consciousness.

You can slow down your mind at any time during your day, for example at work or in social situations. Simply close your eyes and become mindful of your breathing. If you notice that you are breathing quickly or taking shallow breaths, consciously breathe in and out slowly and deeply. Mentally draw the downward arc of a circle as you slowly breathe in, and an upward arc of a circle as you slowly breathe out.

Continue doing this until you feel centered—this may take about a minute. This Awareness Centering Technique is also very effective in helping you go to sleep, or go back to sleep at night, since it frees your mind of distracting thoughts.

3. The Visual Centering Technique

In this technique you focus on a visual image such as a "mandala." Mandala is a Sanskrit word meaning "to have possession of one's essence," and a mandala is a mesmerizing shape which is geometrically designed to focus your mind. The Tibetan word for mandala means "the center of the universe in which a fully awakened being abides." Dr. Patricia Garfield writes that "mandalas are meaningful, organized structures, not merely concentric drawings or decorative formal designs. They convey, in a pictographic way, whole philosophical systems, entire bodies of knowledge. Every detail within a mandala is symbolically significant."[67] Mandalas allow us to access our inner world since they are the keys that unlock the mysteries of our soul's architecture.

In the West, Carl Jung was influential in showing how mandalas relate to our psyches and dreams as we undertake the adventure through which each individual explores his or her own unconscious. "The ultimate goal of such a search is the forming of a harmonious and balanced relationship with the Self. The circular mandala images the perfect balance."[68] Jung believed that mandalas are "vessels" into which we project our psyches. He discovered that his clients experienced circular images as a "movement toward psychological growth, expressing the idea of a safe refuge, inner reconnection and wholeness."

In Eastern philosophies, the mandala is a symbol for the Wheel of Life, which represents universal spiritual laws and their applications in ethical conduct. You do not have to look to the East for examples of mandalas, since they are found throughout creation. Examples of the mandala pattern are found in the atomic pattern at the tip of a platinum needle (see Figure B.1.) and in liquid created by harmonic vibrations (see Figure B.2.).

Atomic pattern at the tip of a platinum needle
(enlarged 750,000 times)

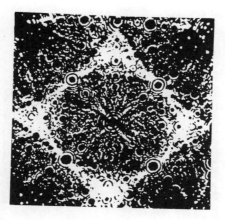

Figure B.1.

Pattern in liquid created by harmonic vibrations

Figure B.2.

For the *Visual Centering Technique* you can use the circular image of a thistle flower. (See Figure B.3.) Begin this technique by placing the picture of this, or any mandala of your choice, a short distance in front of you, at eye level. Focus your awareness on the entire mandala by looking at it steadily while you continue to breathe slowly and deeply. After a while your mind will let go of its stream of thoughts and you will experience "one–pointed concentration," where your total awareness is of the mandala. You may also experience a sense of merging with the mandala, so that the dichotomy of your awareness and the picture, subject and object, no longer exists. You and your inner awareness become one.

Mandala Pattern of a Thistle Flower

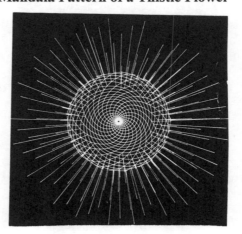

Figure B.3.

If during this process your mind begins to wander or your thoughts come back, focus consciously on the center of the mandala, continue to breathe deeply, and let your thoughts go. After a while your attention will expand back to the whole mandala.

Continue concentrating on the mandala in this way for 20 minutes. After doing this technique, you should feel a more focused, clear consciousness, which will last for a period of time.

If you like this technique and want other mandalas to look at, I recommend the book *Mandalas of the World* by Rudiger Dahlke as a wonderful guide for visual centering.[69]

Notes

1. Paul H. Ray, "The Rise of Integral Culture," *Noetic Sciences Review*, Spring 1996, pp. 4-15.
2. Carl Sagan, *Cosmos* (New York: Random House, 1980), p. 345.
3. Paul H. Ray, "The Rise of Integral Culture."
4. John Grinnell, Jr., *Quality Progress*, November 1994.
5. Carl C. Jung, *Man And His Symbols* (New York: Dell Publishing, 1964), p. 174.
6. Andrew P. Morrison, M.D., *Culture of Shame* (New York:Ballantine Books, 1996).
7. Alan Richardson, *Research Quarterly*.
8. Maxwell Maltz, M.D.,*Psycho-Cybernetics* (New York: Pocket Books, 1971), p. 13.
9. Ibid., p. 12.
10. Bertrand Russell, *The Autobiography of Bertrand Russell* (Boston: Little, Brown and Company, 1967), p. 3.
11. Paul Davies, *The Cosmic Blueprint: New Discoveries in Nature's Creative Ability to Order the Universe* (New York/London: Simon & Schuster, 1992), p. 138.
12. James Gleick, *Chaos* (New York: Viking, 1988), p. 6.
13. Richard Grossinger, *Embryogesis* (Berkeley: North Atlantic Books,1986) pp. 70-71.
14. James Gleick, *Chaos*, p. 6.
15. Fritjof Capra, *The Web Of Life* (New York: Doubleday, 1996), p. 96.
16. David R. Goldberg, David R. Rigney, and Bruce J. West, "Chaos and Fractals in Human Physiology," *Scientific American*, February 1990, p. 49.
17. James Gleick, *Chaos*, p. 5.
18. Erich Jantsch, *Design for Evolution: Self-Organizing and Planning in Life and Human Systems* (New York: G. Braziller, 1975), p. 289.
19. Menas Kafatos and Robert Nadeau, *The Conscious Universe* (New York: Springer-Verlag, 1994), p. 127.
20. Ibid., p. 128.
21. George Doczi, *The Power of Limits* (Boston: Shambhala,1985), p. 1.
22. *The Random House Encyclopedia* (New York: Random House,1990, p. 1485.
23. Fritjof Capra, *The Tao of Physics* (New York: Bantam New Age, 1984), p. 50.
24. Daniel McNeill & Paul Freiberger, *Fuzzy Logic* (New York: Simon & Schuster, 1993), p. 28.
25. Bart Kosko and Satoru Iska, "Fuzzy Logic," *Scientific American*, July 1993, p. 80.

208

Notes

26. Ibid., p. 76.
27. Erich Jantsch, *The Self-Organizing Universe* (New York: Grove Press, Inc., 1974), p. 274.
28. Walpolal Rahula, *What The Buddha Taught* (New York: Grove Press, 1974), p. 45.
29. Chogyam Trungpa, *Cutting Through Spiritual Materialism* (Berkeley: Shambala, 1973), p. 20.
30. Riane Eisler, *The Chalice and the Blade* (New York: Harpe Collins, 1995) and Paul H. Ray, "The Rise of Integral Culture."
31. Leonard Shlain, *The Alphabet Versus The Goddess* (New York: Penguin Putnam,1998), pp. 7–24.
32. Antonio R. Damasio, "The Emotional Brain," *Scientific American*, June, 1997.
33. John G. Neilhart, *Black Elk Speaks* (New York: Pocket Books, Simon & Schuster, 1972), pp. 164-165.
34. *The Random House Encyclopedia*, p. 820.
35. Malcolm Cowley, *The Portable Emerson* (New York: Penguin Books, 1981), p. 227.
36. *The Mind/Body Workbook,* New England Deaconess Hospital, Boston, MA.
37. Herbert Benson, M.D., *The Relaxation Response* (New York: Avon Books, 1975)
38. Carl C. Jung, *Man And His Symbols* (New York: Dell Publishing, 1964), p. 267.
39. Ibid., p. 384.
40. Teilhard de Chardin, *The Divine Milieu* (Harper & Row: New York, 1965); Thomas Berry, *The Dream of the Earth* (Sierra Club Books: San Francisco, 1988); Matthew Fox, *The Coming of the Cosmic Christ* (Harper & Row: San Francisco, 1988); Ramon G. Mendoza, Ph.D, *The Acentric Labyrinth* (Rockport, MA: Element Books, Inc., 1995).
41. Emily Preston, *Stony Brook Wildlife Sanctuary,* Spring, 1989.
42. Brian Swimme, *The Universe Is a Green Dragon: A Cosmic Creation Story* (Santa Fe: Bear & Co., 1984), p. 18.
43. Menas Kafatos and Robert Nadeau, *The Conscious Universe*, p. 176.
44. Fritjof Capra, *The Tao of Physics*, p. 57.
45. Fritjof Capra, *The Turning Point* (New York: Bantam, 1982), p. 78.
46. Paul Davies, *The Cosmic Blueprint: New Discoveries in Nature's Creative Ability to Order the Universe*, p. 210.
47. Paul Davies, *God and the New Physics* (New York: Simon &Schuster, 1983), p. 210.
48. Erich Jantsch, *The Self-Organizing Universe*, last page, quoted in Matthew Fox audiocassette, *The Cosmic Christ*.
49. David Bohm, *Revision*, Summer/Fall Quarterly, p. 177.

Notes

50. Russ Dicarlo, Interview with Joan Borysenko, "Towards a New World View," *Earth Star*, October/November, p. 41.
51. Matthew Fox, *The Coming of the Cosmic Christ* (San Francisco: Harper & Row, 1988), p. 57.
52. *The 1993 Information Please Environmental Almanac,* compiled by World Resources Institute (Boston & New York: Houghton Mifflin, 1993).
53. Brian Swimme, *Spirituality of the Universe: Canticle to the Cosmos*, video series.
54. Brian Swimme, *The Hidden Heart of the Cosmos: Humanity and the New Story* (Maryknoll, N.Y: Orbis Books, 1996), p. 17.
55. David Bellamy and Brendan Quale, *Turning the Tide* (London: William Collins & Sons,1986 , p. 41.
56. Jacques–Yves Cousteau, Foreward, *The Home Planet*, ed. Kevin W. Kelly (Reading, MA and Moscow: Addison–Wesley and Mir Publishing, 1988).
57. Kevin W. Kelly, ed., *The Home Planet*, p. 70.
58. Ibid., p. 71.
59. Ibid., p. 136.
60. Ibid., p. 24.
61. Ibid., p. 38.
62. Ibid., p. 60.
63. Ibid., p. 77.
64. Ibid., p. 85.
65. Ibid., p. 85.
66. Ibid., p. 109.
67. Patricia Garfield, Ph.D., *Pathway to Ecstasy* (New York: Prentice Hall Press, 1979), p. 2.
68. Carl C. Jung, *Man and His Symbols*, p. 231.
69. Rudiger Dahlke, *Mandalas of the World: A Meditating and Painting Guide* (New York: Sterling Publishing Co., 1992).

Bibliography

Barlow, Connie. *From Gaia to Selfish Genes*. Cambridge: The MIT Press, 1992.

Bellamy, David and Brendan Quale. *Turning the Tide*. London: William Collins Sons & Co., 1986.

Benoit, Hubert. *Zen and the Psychology of Transformation*. Rochester: Inner Traditions, 1990.

Benson, Herbert M.D. *The Relaxation Response*. New York: Avon Books, 1975.

Berry, Thomas. *The Dream of the Earth*. Sierra Club Books: San Francisco, 1988.

Blakney, Raymond B. *Meister Eckhart.* (New York: Harper Torchbooks, 1941.)

Bohm, David. *Wholeness and the Implicate Order.* Boston: Ark Paperbooks, 1983.

Briggs, John and David Peat. *The Turbulent Mirror: An Illustrated Guide to Chaos Theory and the Science of Wholeness.* New York: Harper & Row, 1989.

Bucke, Maurice Richard, M.D. *Cosmic Consciousness.* Seacaucus: Citadel Press, 1977.

Campbell, Joseph. *The Power of Myths.* New York: Doubleday, 1988.

Capra, Fritjof. *The Tao of Physics.* New York: Bantam New Age, 1984.

Capra, Fritjof. *The Web of Life.* New York: Doubleday, 1996.

Clark, W. Ronald. *Einstein: The Life and Times.* New York: The World Publishing Company, 1971.

Cowley, Malcolm. *The Portable Emerson.* New York: Penguin Books,1981.

Dahlke, Rudiger. *Mandalas of the World.* New York: Sterling Publishing, 1992.

Damasio, Antonio R. *Descartes' Error.* New York: G.P. Putnam's, 1994.

Davies, Paul. *God and the New Physics.* New York: Simon & Schuster, 1983.

Davies, Paul. *The Cosmic Blueprint.* New York/London: Simon & Schuster, 1992.

Doczi, George. *The Power of Limits.* Boston: Shambhala, 1985.

Ellen, Mary and Lucas Ellen. *Teilhard: the Man, the Priest, the Scientist.* New York: Doubleday and Company, 1977.

Ferguson, Marilyn. *The Aquarian Conspiracy.* Los Angeles: J. P. Tarcher, 1980.

Ferris, Timothy. *The Whole Shebang.* New York: Touchstone,1997.

Fox, Matthew. *The Coming of the Cosmic Christ.* San Francisco: Harper & Row, 1988.

Garfield, Patricia, Ph.D. *Pathway to Ecstasy: The Way of the Dream Mandala.* New York: Prentice Hall Press, 1989.

Goodenough, Ursula. *The Sacred Depths of Nature.* New York: Oxford Press, 1998.

Goswami, Amit, Ph.D. *The Self-Aware Universe.* New York: Jeremy P. Tarcher, 1995.

Grof, Stanislav. *Ancient Wisdom and Modern Science.* Albany: State University of New York Press, 1984.

Haeri, Fadhlalla Shaykh. *The Journey of the Self.* New York: Harper Collins, 1991.

Huxley, Aldous. *The Perennial Philosophy.* New York: Harper Colophon, 1945.

Jung, Carl C. *Man and His Symbols.* New York: Dell Publishing,1964.

Jung, Carl C. , ed. R.F.C.Hull. *Mandala Symbolism.* Princeton: Princeton University Press, 1973.

Jantsch, Erich. *The Self-Organizing Universe.* New York: Grove Press, Inc., 1974.

Jantsch, Erich. *Design for Evolution: Self-Organizing and Planning in Life and Human Systems.* New York: G. Braziller, 1975.

Kafatos, Menas and Robert Nadeau. *The Conscious Universe.* New York: Springer-Verlag, 1994

Kelly, Kevin, W. *The Home Planet.* Reading, MA and Moscow: Addison-Wesley and Mir Publishers, 1988.

Leonard, Linda Schierse. *Witness to the Fire of Creativity and the Veil of Addiction.* Boston: Shambhala, 1990.

Bibliography

Margulis, Lynn. *Symbiotic Planet*. Basic Books: New York, 1998.

Mendoza, G. Ramon, Ph.D. *The Acentric Labyrinth*. Rockport: Element Books, 1995.

McNeill, Daniel and Paul Freiberger. *Fuzzy Logic*. New York: Simon & Schuster, 1993.

Morrison, Andrew P. M..D. *Culture of Shame*. New York: Ballantine Books, 1996.

Needleman, Jacob. *A Sense of the Cosmos*. New York: Arkana Paperbacks, 1975.

Neilhart, G. John. *Black Elk Speaks*. New York: Pocket Books, Simon & Schuster, 1972.

Revel, Jean-Francois and Ricard Matthieu. *The Monk and the Philosopher*. New York: Schocken Books, 1999.

Rahula, Walpolal. *What the Buddha Taught*. New York: Grove Press, 1974.

Sagan, Carl. *Billions & Billions*. New York: Ballantine Books, 1997.

Sagan, Carl. *Cosmos*. New York: Random House, 1980.

Schneider, S. Michael. *A Beginner's Guide to Constructing the Universe*. New York: Harper Collins, 1994.

Shlain, Leonard. *The Alphabet Versus the Goddess*. New York: Penguin Putnam, 1998.

Swimme, Brian. *The Universe Is a Green Dragon: A Cosmic Creation Story*. Santa Fe: Bear & Co., 1984.

Swimme, Brian. *The Hidden Heart of the Cosmos: Humanity and the New Story*. Maryknoll, N.Y: Orbis Books, 1996.

Trungpa, Chogyam. *Cutting Through Spiritual Materialism*. Berkeley: Shambhala, 1973.

Von Bertalanffy, Ludwig. *The Model of Open Systems*. New York: Braziller, 1968.

Walsh, Roger N., Ph.D and Frances Vaughan, Ph.D. *Beyond Ego*. Los Angeles: J.P. Tarcher, 1980.

Welwood, John. *Awakening the Heart*. Boulder: Shambhala, 1983.

Wheatley, Margaret. *Leadership and the New Sciences*. San Francisco: Berrett-Koehler, 1994.

Wilber, Ken. *A Brief History of Everything*. Boston: Shambhala, 1996.

Wolf, Fred Alan, Ph.D. *The Spiritual Universe*. New York: Simon & Schuster, 1996.

If you want to learn more
about how to apply the Balanced Paradigm
in your personal and professional life....

JACK BEAUREGARD, author of ***The Power of Balance***, and an inspirational lecturer, experienced seminar leader, and successful company CEO, offers lectures, workshops and seminars on how to apply the principles and process of the Balanced Paradigm for:

- Personal transformation
- Organizational transformation
- Professional development

Now you can bring the dynamic, inspiring yet down–to–earth message and style from *The Power of Balance* to your organization or workplace, with one or more exciting presentations by author, seminar leader, and successful CEO Jack Beauregard (see descriptions below).

Jack is founder and President of Innervisions Associates, founder and former President of a national multi-million dollar orthopedic products firm. He studied Comparative Religions at the Harvard Divinity School in order to integrate spirituality and science.

Jack Beauregard's speaking presentations are enlightening and inspirational. His effective programs, based on many years as a public speaker and seminar leader, show audiences how to

Call 1-888-617-6715   jack@thepowerofbalance.com

create balance, fulfillment, and meaning in both their personal and professional lives. Jack is a great motivator since he speaks to both the heads and the hearts of audiences.

Since 1980, Jack Beauregard has presented Seminars, Conference Keynotes and Lectures, and In–house Workshops in Professional Development and Organizational Transformation for businesses, professionals, and their associations, including:

- American Society for Training and Development
- Software development professionals
- Employee Assistance Professionals
- Psychiatrists and Pastoral Counselors
- Licensed social workers and other mental health professionals
- Community mental health staff
- Elementary and secondary school teachers, principals, and administrators
- Hospital administrators and managed care professionals
- National sales meetings
- and more

Jack Beauregard has also presented workshops on Personal Transformation at educational centers including the New York City Learning Annex, the Boston Learning Society, and the Boston Theological Library, and he has been a guest speaker on Cable TV and on Dr. T. Berry Brazelton's national TV program "American Family Album."

Call 1-888-617-6715   jack@thepowerofbalance.com

Feedback from Jack Beauregard's Presentations and Workshops:

"One of the more pleasurable parts of my job as Program Chair is recruiting dynamic presenters for our monthly meetings. Never was this more true than for our January meeting. Jack Beauregard's presentation was truly one of the more exiting and stimulating meetings of my tenure. I thank Jack for his outstanding presentation and contribution of time, energy, and imagination, which resulted in that program being one of the best we've ever presented."

Henry E. Culver, Ed.D. Program Chair,
American Society for Training and Development

"I want to thank Jack Beauregard for the informative workshop he did in the Learning Annex in New York City. I wish Jack much success in communicating his ideas to people throughout the country. He's a wonderful communicator and keeps an audience interested."

Laurie Cagnassola, New York City Learning Annex

"It was a delight to meet Jack and a pleasure to do a show with him. He did a wonderful job sharing his life and the principles of joyful living. I know his story will touch many hearts."

Vera Armen,"Alive! Body, Mind & Spirit," Boston– area TV program

Feedback from Jack Beauregard/Innervisions Associates Seminars on Organizational Transformation:

"This program was a great way to spur everyone to creative thinking by providing a forum for us to offer ideas. It also got us thinking and communicating—allowed people to open up."

Steve Harris, Company President, Information Resource Systems

"Sensible and direct."   Bob Cohen, Business Development

Call 1-888-617-6715   jack@thepowerofbalance.com

"Great communication vehicle for those within our organization. The workshop helped us to move forward."

Brad Sweet, Product Development Manager

"I enjoyed the interactive exercises. They forced you to think about the situation at hand and actually develop a structured plan for what needs to be done.

Jane Anastasi, Marketing

"This seminar established a framework which allowed us to broaden our thinking about change."

Paula Labbe, Secretary

"There are very powerful concepts behind the 'Balanced Paradigm' model which were reinforced by props, visual aids, and exercises."

Ken Halkin, MBA,
Vice-President, Tri–City Mental Health Centers

JACK BEAUREGARD: PROGRAMS FOR PERSONAL TRANSFORMATION

THE POWER OF BALANCE: HOW TO STAY ON COURSE THROUGH LIFE'S UPS AND DOWNS

This workshop presents a practical, innovative approach to helping you stay on course through the ups and downs of everyday life. Through four core principles which integrate the wisdom of the world's great spiritual traditions with the latest findings of modern science, Jack

Call 1-888-617-6715   jack@thepowerofbalance.com

Beauregard, author of *The Power of Balance: Seven Principles for Transforming Mind, Spirit, and Self* will show you how to connect to your inner psychological Center of Balance. You will then discover how to use this centering point to:

- Grow beyond limiting beliefs and self-defeating habits
- Enhance your decision making ability
- Balance and ground your life
- Transform any negative situation into a positive outcome

BLESSINGS FOR THE 21st CENTURY: A NEW BALANCED MODEL FOR LIVING

Experience a sense of sacredness in your everyday world. Through three grounded spiritual principles which integrate the wisdom of the world's great spiritual traditions with the latest findings of modern science, Jack Beauregard, author of *The Power of Balance: Seven Principles for Transforming Mind, Spirit, and Self* will show you how to access your spiritual center and enable you to experience inner wisdom and unconditional love on a daily basis. The principles in this workshop will help you to:

- Fill your life with meaning and purpose
- Feel guided in everyday life
- Enhance your creative and intuitive abilities
- Create harmony in all your relationships
- Expand your awareness to a higher level of consciousness

Call 1-888-617-6715   jack@thepowerofbalance.com

JACK BEAUREGARD / INNERVISIONS ASSOCIATES PROGRAMS FOR PROFESSIONAL DEVELOPMENT

WHY "POSITIVE THINKING" DOES NOT WORK--AND WHAT DOES!

Find out why Dale Carnegie could not write the last chapter in his famous book, *How to Make Friends and Influence People,* and why Norman Vincent Peale and the other preachers of the "Gospel of Positive Thinking" cannot answer why we continue to do things that we don't understand and why we cannot create balance in our lives.

In this workshop, through four core principles which integrate the wisdom of the world's great spiritual traditions with the latest findings of modern science, Jack Beauregard, author of *The Power of Balance: Seven Principles for Transforming Mind, Spirit, and Self* will show you how to move beyond seeing the world from only a black and white perspective and expand your framework for thinking, problem-solving, and action, by learning how to use the negatives in your life :

- As catalysts for personal growth
- To balance and create wholeness in your life
- To create genuine positive alternatives

Jack Beauregard and Innervisions Associates also offer the following SEMINARS IN PROFESSIONAL DEVELOPMENT based on the principles of the Balanced Paradigm. These programs provide transformational solutions for you and your staff in the following areas:

Call 1-800-617-6715   sales@thepowerofbalance.com

- ▸ From Outer Chaos to Inner Balance: How to Deal with Non–Stop Changes in the Workplace

- ▸ Yes! Let's Work Together: Creating Effective Cooperation and Productive Teamwork

- ▸ Enhancing Energy in Your Workplace: How to Enhance Employee Commitment

- ▸ Strategic Creativity: How to Increase Employee Creativity

All Innervisions Professional Development Seminars utilize lectures, visual aids, interactive exercises, and participatory discussions to energize participants and enhance their learning and creativity.

We can also develop customized programs for your specific organizational needs. For more information see our website, www.thepowerofbalance.com.

JACK BEAUREGARD / INNERVISIONS ASSOCIATES BUSINESS TRANSFORMATIONAL PROGRAMS

Jack Beauregard and his company, Innervisions Associates, offer workshops and seminars for businesses and non-profit workplaces seeking a better method for strengthening company coherence and dealing with internal and external change.

Here are some of our offerings. For more details see our

website, www.thepowerofbalance.com..We can also develop customized programs for your specific organizational needs.

A NEW INTEGRATED SUCCESS MODEL FOR DOING BUSINESS

This seminar gives your entire organization an intense introduction to the universal principles derived from the latest discoveries from psychology and mainstream leading edge astronomy, physics, and systems theory. These principles create a new model for doing business—the Balanced Business Paradigm which:

Supports employees full use of their potential by helping them:
- Become genuinely positive
- Expand their thinking to a balanced perspective
- Focus their personal energies
- Transform negative experiences into positive outcomes

Enhances the effectiveness of teams/workgroups by showing how to:
- Create a positive, productive team environment
- Find both the techniques for creative solutions and the skills to implement them
- Adopt new leadership skills for the new millennium
- Develop effective team decision–making skills

Brings your company to its optimal level of performance by:
- Providing a framework for greater inter–team and interdepartmental cooperation
- Creating a congruency between the company's core principles, values, and actions
- Expanding the organization to an integrated, living model Creating a long–term, wholistic perspective
- Creating a focused approach to an ever–changing business environment

Call 1-800-677-6715   sales@thepowerofbalance.com

HIGHER LEVEL OF BUSINESS CONSCIOUSNESS: CONNECTING WITH THE CORE OF YOUR ORGANIZATION

Seven core principles of the universe recently discovered by science, create the framework for a new business model, the Balanced Paradigm, which naturally expands the consciousness of business.

The Power of Balance that is unleashed through this new integrated business model applies the evolutionary force of the universe to business growth, while changing the "consciousness" of the organization—the mental attitudes and beliefs of the people within the company—which is the key to creating meaningful, permanent change. This transformative process breaks through limiting business beliefs and self defeating habits. It expands an organization's inner awareness which allows a business to connect with its core, its organizational "Center of Balance." This allows a business to access its deepest principles and values, and turn them into practical, effective action.

This revolutionary program of organizational transformation creates a new way of business thinking, based on a new logic system, that fosters balanced decision making and expands the awareness of business organizations to a higher level of consciousness which:

- Develops the ability to turn negative situations into positive outcomes
- Helps you stay focused in the midst of unprecedented change
- Promotes organizational creativity
- Transforms human relationships within the organization
- Creates a positive, spirited work environment
- Allows your business to connect to the very core from which its values emerge
- Awakens the spiritual dimension of your business
- Enriches the bottom line by enriching the souls of your employees
- Creates congruence between spirit and your professional life
- Supports social and environmental responsibility

Call 1-800-677-6715   sales@thepowerofbalance.com